THAT COULD NEVER BE

Kevin Dalton

That Could Never Be

A MEMOIR

with Patrick Semple

With very best wishes

Kevin Dalton

the columba press

First published in 2003 by
the columba press
55A Spruce Avenue, Stillorgan Industrial Park,
Blackrock, Co Dublin

Reprinted 2003

Cover by Bill Bolger
Origination by The Columba Press
Printed in Ireland by ColourBooks Ltd, Dublin

ISBN 1 85607 393 9

Acknowledgements
I wish to thank the following for help willingly given: Liz Neill-Watson,
Hilary Semple, Carole Cullen, Leo Cullen, Nan Dwyer and Dan Swift.
Some names have been changed to preserve anonymity.

Contents

Grow old along with me!
The best is yet to be,
The last of life, for which the first was made:
Our times are in His hand
Who saith 'A whole I planned,
Youth shows but half; trust God: see all, nor be afraid!'

Robert Browning
Rabbi Ben Ezra

Preface

I first met Kevin Dalton in a pub in Donnybrook late one winter Saturday afternoon in 1958. He had come there to meet a friend who had been playing rugby. I cannot remember anything that passed between us that day. Subsequently I met him at occasional parties, usually late on Saturday night or early Sunday morning, around the Rathmines and Rathgar area of Dublin. From time to time we bumped into each other in College Street or Hawkins Street on the way to work, he on his way to the Dublin Port Mill down the quays and I going in the opposite direction on my way from Tara Street station to College Green. We never stopped but exchanged greetings or comments as we passed, because Kevin was always late.

In the summer of 1961 at a dinner dance in the Gresham Hotel Kevin came up to me and said: 'I hear you're going to CACTM.' (A Church of Ireland ordination selection conference.)

'I am,' I said, not having any idea how he knew.

'So am I.' This was the first time I had any inclination that he was planning to be ordained.

Kevin and I travelled together to the conference in County Down. I certainly was glad of the company, and I think he was too. It seemed to me that he comported himself over those three days with great confidence. He had a natural, and often humorous, way of interacting with people that was winning, but he also had the opposite facility when he wanted to use it: he could close out people if he didn't want to interact.

After that conference we were both approved for training for ordination and Kevin entered Trinity in the autumn. I entered the following year. We saw each other from time to time during that year and we had long telephone conversations. Kevin would phone casually for a chat any time between 11.00 pm and 12.00 midnight. I am normally in bed by 11 o'clock so more often than not these calls woke me. At first I said nothing, then suggested that he phone a little earlier, and finally told him in no uncertain terms not to phone after 11 o'clock. All of this was to no avail, so I phoned him one morning at 7.00 am.

'What's wrong?' he asked.

'Nothing,' I said, 'I've just phoned for a chat.' I won't recount what he said, but the late night calls stopped!

One evening during my first year in college Kevin, with that characteristic beckoning by an inclination of the head, called me aside and asked me to go for a drink. When we sat down he told me his story. I had thought much of him up to this, but having heard his story my admiration for him was huge and I told him so. When I told him how much I admired what he had achieved, he grinned and shrugged his shoulders as if to say:

'I don't see anything special in it.'

What Kevin told me that night was just an outline of his life and over the years he recounted bits and pieces, usually because they were humorous. It is remarkable that there was never an iota of self-pity, and as George Simms once said to him:

'There's no bitterness.'

Forty years after he first confided in me, on the way home from a couple of days together in the West of Ireland, I said to Kevin:

'Why don't you write your story?'

'Why?' he said, 'Who'd be interested?' and he meant it. He had always maintained his life was very ordinary. After much persuasion on my part he said:

'OK, I'll tell you what I'll do. I'll tell it if you'll write it.'

At first Kevin did not take the project seriously. Often he wouldn't have time to give me the next instalment on tape:

'I'm too busy in the parish. It's all right for you, you've nothing else to do. Who's going to be interested anyway?' Eventually he gave me most of his story on tape which Liz Neill-Watson, his secretary, transcribed. From these transcripts I did what I could to put order and context on it. When the first draft was finished he read it through. It was accepted for publication on that first draft and this gave him confidence that his story was worth telling. He then began to work at it in earnest, always subject to his work in the parish. He revised the draft and he gave me more material to add. After further revisions and additions what follows is the result.

Patrick Semple

CHAPTER ONE

Beginnings

The year was 1932. The Lindberg baby was kidnapped in America, The Nazis became the largest party in Germany, the Eucharistic Congress took place in Dublin and the Roman Catholic Church was in firm control, not only of the lives of 90 to 95% of the population but of the State itself. It was the year that the Republican Party, Fianna Fáil, took power for the first time after the Civil War of only ten years before and it was the year that I was born. In Ireland unemployment was rife, poverty abounded and the economic war with Britain was starting to depress agriculture, potentially our best industry. Only a small number of people owned cars, and horses and carts were common on the streets of Dublin. Many homes did not have a wireless and the arrival of television in Ireland was twenty years into the future.

My earliest memory is of being restrained in my movement by something I was wearing, presumably a nappy, outside a small house set back from the footpath just beyond Leonard's Corner on the South Circular Road. I have the impression that my mother was working at the time and somebody was looking after me. I must have been about two. Another early memory was of being pushed along Castlewood Avenue, Rathmines in a go-car with another child and while whoever was pushing us had stopped to talk to another person a dog came along and jumped up and licked my face. I have a vivid memory of the terror I felt and the consternation the dog caused. I wouldn't have been more than three at the time.

An outstanding memory of four or so years later was going to Leeson Park Church on a Sunday morning. It was pouring

rain. 'Daddy' Hughes was the rector and the new Archbishop of
Dublin Dr Barton was to preach. Whoever was with me stopped
to talk to somebody who said gravely, 'War has been declared.'
The tone in which it was said made a lasting impression on me.
That, as I learned later, was 3 September 1939. I remember too,
early in the war, when bombs fell on North Strand. I was in an
orphanage in Northbrook Road and all of us children had been
in bed. We were brought downstairs to the window of one of the
front rooms from where we saw red tracers in the sky. I remember two planes and loud explosions.

I was born in September in Dublin in the old Coombe Lying-
in Hospital. The portico and front steps are all that are left of the
old hospital and when I pass them I think of the generations of
women of all sorts and conditions leaving hospital with their
new babies facing out into the world. My mother, Nellie, came
down those steps with me and out into, for her, a very uncertain
world. She wasn't married and so I was given her surname
name, Dalton.

To be born out of wedlock in Catholic Ireland of the 1930s
was not, to say the least, a promising start. In those days it was a
tough world: it was particularly tough for a young woman without means to be faced with the birth of a baby outside marriage.
I don't know how she coped, and I have no idea what her relationship with her family was. I do know, however, that she
brought me to that beautiful Roman Catholic church, St
Nicholas of Myra in Francis Street, where I was baptised.
According to my baptismal certificate a woman by the name of
Agnes was my godmother. Some fifty years later I was invited to
take part in the wedding of two Roman Catholic friends in that
church when I had the opportunity to appreciate its beauty. It
was, for me, an emotional occasion.

My mother lived in a flat in Patrick Street in the south inner
city. I believe she worked as a housemaid. She must have been a
strong-willed woman, for all the signs are that she was determined to keep her baby. Having me in the Coombe Hospital and
arranging for me to be baptised in a parish church would not

have been the usual procedure for an unmarried working-class mother of the time. Birth and baptism in the circumstances would normally have taken place in a Magdalen Home. I do know that within two months of my birth she moved with me into the Bethany Home, a Protestant mother and baby home where we stayed until the end of the following March. Then it seems that a Mrs McCoy, who lived in a house near Leonard's Corner, looked after me while my mother worked.

I have a letter from my mother from an address in Raglan Road, Ballsbridge to a Miss Walker of the Bethany Home, when I was two. She enclosed twelve shillings and sixpence off her bill with the home. She recounts that on the previous night she had spoken to Miss Carr who told her there was a waiting list of little boys and the Board would make the decision on Kevin the following week. In the letter my mother pleads with Miss Walker to use her influence with Miss Carr to get me into Miss Carr's Home. She says she is aware that Miss Carr hasn't many places but 'I am going more into debt every month as I have so much to do with my few shillings I do not know what way to turn.' She hopes that with Miss Walker's influence I will be accepted. If not, she says, 'I will try to get a place where I can keep him myself.'

Miss Walker was apparently successful as I was placed in Miss Carr's Home in 1934. My mother, a Roman Catholic, despite the fact that she had me baptised in a Catholic church, appears to have made a conscious decision to place me in a Protestant rather than a Roman Catholic home. The situation for an unmarried woman having a baby in those days was desperate. When it came to dealing with women pregnant outside marriage, condemnation rather than holiness or Christian compassion was the norm. This would have been, to a large extent, the attitude of people of all religions.

In my case my mother opted for a Protestant home with a good reputation where she knew her child would be cared for and loved, I believe in the hope of being able to take me back again in the future when she got on her feet. This came at the price of surrendering for me her faith which may well have been the only thing that kept her going. This must have been an awful decision. I have no doubt that she did, in the circumstances, what she believed was the best thing for me.

In October 1887 Miss Lizzie Hawthorn Carr opened a home at 25 Nelson Street, Dublin, for destitute children. Between then and 1932 she had a number of homes throughout the city. By 1932 when she died, all of Miss Carr's Homes' children, approximately thirty, were accommodated at No 5 Northbrook Road. Her cousin Miss Eunice Carr, who was already a member of the staff at the home, succeeded her and continued the tradition of making the love and care of the children her primary concern.

No 5 Northbrook Road was a large, red brick, semi-detached house with stone steps to the hall door. Northbrook Road is off Leeson Park, a professional or upper middle-class suburb of South Dublin. To be rector of Leeson Park church in those days would have been the pinnacle of any clergyman's aspirations for a living. We children knew the home as 'No 5'.

The main room off the hall on the righthand side was the playroom. There was lino on the floor, as there was on all the floors. It was here that we spent hours playing our make believe games and playing with what toys there were that had been given to the home for our use. These included a large rocking horse and a vaulting horse that we never used because it was too big. There was a small sitting-room on the right of the hall and behind it a room where some of the staff lived. The dining-room was on the left of the hall and it was from the window of that room that in 1941 we looked up at the sky and saw the planes that bombed North Strand. At the back there were two steps down to the return of the house, with a door to the left onto an outside landing with steps leading down to the garden. One night I stood on those steps with two other boys in a thunder and lightning storm and thought how brave I was and how I was determined to stay there longer than anybody else.

The garden was a favourite place for the boys. In the middle there was a mulberry tree round which we used to sing the children's song 'Here we go round the mulberry bush.' I can remember on more than one occasion when a cat or kitten, to which we had become attached, died, we had a funeral procession and buried it under the tree. I cannot remember who was the clergyman on those occasions, but I was always the undertaker in charge of proceedings.

At the right of the return downstairs there was a staff breakfast room where we were not allowed to go. Beside it was the kitchen with a big black range and off it a pantry that in the autumn was full with fruit and vegetables donated to the home from the Harvest Thanksgiving Services of some Dublin parishes. Upstairs were the bedrooms for the children and Miss Carr's bedroom.

We went to school further up Northbrook Road to the local Church of Ireland National School. On the way we passed an Old Men's Home with bent and crooked old men on sticks walking in the grounds. Mrs Noonan was the school principal and Miss Boyle the assistant teacher. There we mixed with other children from the district and I don't remember anything that marked us out as the children from the orphanage.

I think I was average at school work but I remember when learning addition I knew that the thing to do was get the number under the line right, but I didn't know how. I put any number I thought of at random under the line and one day by chance I got a difficult addition right. Mrs Noonan proclaimed me a mathematical genius, but my reputation was immediately shattered when inevitably my guesses to subsequent sums were wrong. Eventually I caught on to the principle of simple addition and realised that my former right answer had been pure chance. At lunch break one day I went into the schoolroom from the playground to talk to the teachers. They sat me up on a desk with my legs dangling and asked me to sing. When I finished one of them rewarded me with a sandwich. From time to time I offered my services again and was always similarly rewarded.

While I was in Miss Carr's somebody decided I had bandy legs so I was brought to the Adelaide Hospital. One day while I was waiting in the outpatients with dozens of other children, one of the mothers tried to soothe her baby by singing a hymn and to my surprise some of the other women joined in. I was pleased that I could sing too since I knew the hymn: 'Jesus loves me this I know.' There would be a different reaction today if somebody started to sing hymns in a hospital waiting room.

All the staff were caring of the children of No 5. Children used to hang out of Miss Carr making it difficult for her to get on with her work. At one Christmas party I called Miss Carr by her nickname, Shooney Booney, a nickname she didn't like and that we were forbidden to use. Miss Martin, one of the helpers, took the slipper to me and chased me away from the party and up the stairs to the bedroom. I had to stay in bed for the rest of the evening and no amount of crying or pleading could change that decision and allow me back to the party. I was left completely alone and very sorry for myself, and during that long evening I had to listen to the sound of games and music coming from downstairs. I promised myself I would never risk something like that happening again. Miss Bayle was another helper and I was careful never to let her hear me calling her 'Mammy Bale' that we called her amongst ourselves.

In summer we went to a holiday home in Rush or to the Christian Endeavour house in Greystones. We looked forward to this for ages before and the excitement when the day arrived and we went to the station was enormous. Some of the time on the beach was organised, when we played games and ran races, and some of the time we were free to paddle, swim or make sandcastles. In Greystones we were always brought to hear the itinerant preachers, who from time to time appeared on the beach to try to save people's souls.

Some of the members of the Home's Committee came to the Christmas party. One of these, a Mr Hardman, a big man with a beard, used to join in the games. He would catch us and sing:

> Solomon said, of matchless mind,
> Spare the rod and spoil the child.
> Be it man or be it maid
> Whip 'em and wallop 'em
> Solomon said,

and he would give us a playful smack on the bottom.

There was a Pound Day every year. It was an open day when friends and supporters were invited to meet the helpers and children, to look around the home and contribute £1 to the funds. While they drank tea we children did party pieces. I remember standing up on a small platform with a little girl, dressed in our best clothes for our recitation:

> Joan and me went out to tea
> Dressed as nicely as we could be.
> Mummy said as she shook her head
> We must begin with butter and bread.
> But cakes were there … enough and to spare …

and I can't remember the rest, so when I used to say this for my own children years later I would end with 'and so the poor doggie got none' which made them furious, but I simply could not remember any more. I have a strong memory of feeling 'the orphan' when doing these recitations.

I remember clearly my mother coming to the home from time to time in the afternoon and bringing me out to a café for tea and lemonade. She would dip a marshmallow biscuit into her tea, and every time I eat a marshmallow biscuit I think of her. On these visits she used to bring me sweets and sometimes socks that no doubt she had knitted for me herself. Occasionally her sister was with her with her son Michael who was about my own age or a little older. My memory of my mother was that she was tall with dark hair, striking looking rather than pretty. Years later I did trace her birth certificate and my estimate of her age, and that I was born when she was in her early twenties, were right. I also discovered that she was the youngest of eleven children.

One day when I was about seven, Miss Carr told me one of the helpers would help me to wash and dress in my best clothes, as a man and woman, who wanted to adopt a little boy, were coming to meet Wilfrid, one of the other little boys, and me. I wasn't entirely sure of the implications of this but I knew enough to know it was a good thing to happen and that I might be leaving the home and going to live with a family. The way the adults spoke about it I knew it was something to be excited about and so I was excited. Suitably dressed and groomed we were both ready to meet the couple who could alter the course of a little boy's life.

That afternoon I was playing with some of the other children. The couple arrived and Wilfrid was called out first to see them. He was with them for what seemed to me like an age, and when he came out it was my turn to go into the drawing-room to meet them. The man and woman who seemed to me to be very old spoke to me in a friendly way and asked me questions. I felt unsure with them, but answered as best I could. When I came out we were both told to go upstairs and change back into our ordinary clothes and I couldn't wait to get back to the playroom. Later I was looking for Wilfrid and one of the helpers told me that the couple had taken him to live with them in the country. The natural hurt of rejection stayed with me for a while but I soon forgot about it.

After the bombs were dropped on North Strand the home was evacuated to the country. We went to Harcourt Street Station, and there was the train standing at the platform. We piled into the carriage. Such excitement when the whistle blew and the deep slow chugging started as we pulled out. We were not allowed to look out the open window for fear of getting smuts in our eyes, so we sat as still as we were able. We had no idea where we were going but we were overcome with excitement.

Eventually the train stopped at Rathdrum where we were met by a man with a pair of horses pulling a dray with boards on the sides, and two men each driving a pony and trap. One or two of the younger helpers and all of the children were helped onto the dray, while Miss Carr and the other helpers got into the traps. It was a fine sunny day in the early summer as we set off into the country on the dray on rough stony roads, not knowing what lay ahead. After a long drive we arrived at the small village of Greenane. We went over a bridge and turned right. Ahead we soon saw a large entrance gate with a gate-lodge. At the gate a woman wearing a black dress to her ankles emerged from the lodge and opened the gate. She smiled up at us and we all waved back.

We drove up the avenue that seemed to go on for ever, with rhododendrons blooming on both sides, and emerged into spacious gardens of cultivated lawns and shrubs and a big house. There was a portico with columns in front of the hall-door and beside the near end of the house, which was curved, there was a clock tower. To the side of that was a large greenhouse behind which ran a series of yard buildings and out-houses. I had never seen anything like it. The driver drove around to the back of the house and deposited us in the yard, at what turned out to be the servants' quarters.

The house was Ballinacor, the home of Captain and Mrs Kemmis, who had agreed to take the children of Miss Carr's Home while there was danger from bombing in Dublin. They were an Anglo-Irish gentry family responding to government requests to do what they could to help with problems the war created. The Captain had served with the Inniskillings in India and later in the First World War, in which he had been badly gassed. No doubt he would have served in the Second War if this had not happened. He was of medium height, average build with grey hair and a grey moustache. He wore tweed plus-fours and jacket and always wore a cap. He was fond of shooting and he loved his dogs. He was gentle and quiet-spoken and was a faithful member of his church and parish. Mrs Kemmis was small, little more than five feet, with a round face and short greying hair of no discernable style. She most often wore cardigan, blouse and a tweed skirt. She was a strong and determined woman who was kind in her own way. Captain and Mrs Kemmis had no children.

Everything I saw – the house, the grounds, the farm and how everything worked – fascinated me. Our accommodation in the servants' quarters was spartan but adequate and for the most part we were confined for our play and spare-time activities to the yards and buildings to the back of the house. It was a large estate, mainly of rough hills and forestry with only a few hundred acres of arable land. There was plenty to discover when we explored the trails that led to a lake up in the wooded hills. Along these trails there were ferns and frocken bushes, and the helpers could always tell when some of us children had slipped away to the woods on our own by our black mouths from eating the frockens. Sometimes a few of us would help Mrs Kemmis with little jobs around the place, when she would reward us by taking us down to the farmyard. While she talked to the steward or herdsman we would get the chance to see, and maybe even touch, the sheep or pigs and watch the hens being fed or the cows being milked. It was all a new and wonderful world to us and we loved it.

In the autumn we walked two miles to the nearest Church of Ireland National School in the village of Ballinatone. There was an old caretaker who lived beside the school that I used to talk to, who insisted on calling me 'Cavan'. No matter how hard I tried I could not get her to pronounce my name properly. She was probably from somewhere in the north of the country. On Sundays we went to Ballinatone church which was beside the school. There were plaques on both sides of the Holy Table, with the creed on one and the ten commandments on the other in gold lettering. The rector was Canon Bradley, a lovable old man who used a magnifying glass to read the lessons. I learned years later that he had a glass eye and when he was in charge of his grandchildren and had to leave them alone he would take out his glass eye, put it on the mantelpiece and tell the children to behave as he would be watching them while he was gone.

When I met the Captain or Mrs Kemmis around the place I always talked to them and they always responded in a friendly way. Unknown to any of the other children I used to steal away and press my face against the glass of one of the windows of the drawing-room when I knew that Captain and Mrs Kemmis were inside. They had two big black Labrador dogs called Barney and Chips, but what really attracted me was that they had a pet rabbit, and when I looked in the window I saw it running around on the floor and sometimes it was asleep on the Captain's arm.

Eventually one day, as I had hoped, the Captain came out and brought me in. When I entered the hall I was mesmerised. On the right there was a large timber panelled library. At the far end of the hall a staircase led to a circular gallery under a glass dome. To the left was the drawing-room with fine furniture which I had only been partly able to see from outside. When I entered the drawing-room with the Captain, Barney and Chips came bounding towards me and I played with them on the floor, but the rabbit kept his distance. Captain and Mrs Kemmis talked to me and asked me questions and asked me to sing a hymn for them, which I did. This was the beginning of a bond between us that was to be a major influence on my life. They brought me into the house many more times when I detached myself from the other children and looked through the drawing room window. Slowly I gained the confidence of the rabbit and the height of my ambition was for it to sleep in my arms, which it eventually did.

Later in the autumn the risk of further bombing in Dublin receded. Somebody decided that it was safe for the children of No 5 to return. We all piled onto the big dray and went to Rathdrum station to catch the train for Dublin. I remember the feeling of melancholy that overcame me and I cried on the train journey back to Dublin. As things turned out, my days in Miss Carr's Home were numbered.

The staff members at No 5 were all women and I was now nine years of age. One day, not long after we returned from Ballinacor, I was discovered by a member of staff in a wardrobe with one of the girls of roughly my own age, each trying to advance their knowledge of the other's anatomy. There was consternation. We were both sent to our dormitories in disgrace. There was a palpable atmosphere of something afoot in the home for the next few days. Staff talked in hushed tones when children were about. It was clear that in our innocence we had overstepped the mark. Nobody said anything directly to me of the matter, but hurried arrangements were made to get me out of the place and a week or so later I was despatched to an orphanage in Limerick, the Havergal Boys' Home.

When the day came for me to leave No 5 Miss Carr stood at the door to say good-bye and said: 'Don't forget to read your Bible and say your prayers every day.' One of the staff took me on the bus to Kingsbridge Station where Archdeacon Waller, a tall well-built clergyman dressed in black and wearing gaiters, met us to take me on the train to Limerick. I was distressed at leaving Miss Carr's which had been my home for as long as I could remember and for most of the journey on the train I cried. The Archdeacon did his best to comfort me by playing push ha'penny on the seat and by making pennies disappear, but I was inconsolable.

After I went to Limerick I never saw my mother again. I have no resentment towards her because of the kind of society that Ireland was in those days. There was no room for somebody who made a mistake as she did. There was no second chance. It seems there was no Christian forgiveness for that mistake. You either covered it up and tried to get on with whatever life you could or you were damned. Whatever course her life took it would have been easier for her without me, and she had done all in her power to ensure that I was properly cared for.

CHAPTER TWO

The Havergal

The train journey was interminable and when we arrived in Limerick we walked the short distance across the road from the station to the Havergal Boys' Home, on Reeves Path, No 33 Parnell Street. It was a double-fronted nineteenth century former residence, three storeys over basement with a large space underneath at the front with access for the delivery of turf to the cellar. A high wall surrounded the home. At the front were large double wooden gates, a small side gate for pedestrian entry and a gate-lodge that incorporated the high boundary wall. There was a small garden at the front, and at the back a large return extended into a long garden.

Inside the hall-door the Archdeacon somehow disappeared and left me alone in the hall crying bitterly, when a woman who turned out to be Mrs Forsythe, the housekeeper, arrived on the scene. She was a big woman doubled over with arthritis so that her bottom stuck out. I discovered subsequently that the boys' nickname for her was 'Bummy'. She put her arms around me and gave me a sweet to try to comfort me. It was one of the few small kindnesses I remember from my days in Limerick. I suppose it was to be expected that a home run for older boys by a man would be a tougher regime than a home run and staffed by women for younger children, including girls, but the contrast with Miss Carr's Home was, to say the least, notable. I soon settled in and learned the routine: what was expected and how, for the most part, to keep out of trouble.

When the house was a residence a man called Massey Reeves had owned it and the boys used to say that he died sitting in front of the fire in the drawing-room that was now the dormitory.

Shortly after I came to the Havergal, in the dormitory one night one of the boys was telling how the ghost of Massey Reeves came back from time to time to keep an eye on his house.

'Oh,' said one of the boys, 'I think I see him now, he's moving around the beds.' Another boy said :

'There he is, I see him, he's sitting on the chair beside your bed, Eddie,' and Eddie Harris took a big swing with his fist and nearly broke his arm on the chair.

When I arrived in the Havergal the master who ran the home was Mickey. A Mr Neely, whom we called Bifty, succeeded him. My memories of the Havergal are centred around routines and events and are not in time sequence. The master's accommodation was on the right-hand side of the hall coming in the front door and Bummy's room was on the left. The kitchen was in the basement where we ate at two wooden tables, sitting on long forms. On the other side of the passage from the kitchen there was a cellar for turf for the open fires that provided the only heat in the house. The Master's bedroom was on the first floor, and the boys slept in dormitories. I slept in No 1 dormitory opposite the master's bedroom. Dormitories No 2 and No 3 were on the top floor. No 3 was where all the wet-the-beds slept and beyond it the bathroom. The smell was incredible in No 3 and when we passed through it on the way to the bathroom we held our noses for fear the smell would knock us out.

I soon discovered there was a strong commitment in the Havergal to the old adage, 'Cleanliness is next to godliness.' There were sixteen boys in the home ranging in age from nine to sixteen, some were orphans like myself and some from broken homes. One of our jobs was to keep the home clean by scrubbing it down three or four times a week. On these days we got up at six thirty, summer or winter, and scrubbed down the whole house. The buckets and brushes were kept in a storeroom in the basement, and we trooped out to the garden to collect the floor-cloths from where they had been left on the rockery the day before. We filled the buckets with cold water and scrubbed and washed our way through the dormitories, along the landings and down the stairs and through the schoolroom, kitchen and pantries. In winter the floorcloths were often frozen stiff when we collected them and in really cold weather the water sometimes froze on the stone-flagged floors in the basement. While we were at this work fights broke out easily if anyone was judged by the others not to be doing his fair share of the work. One winter's morning an awful row broke out between Georgie Brown and Billy Thomas, which ended up with Thomas emptying a bucket of dirty water over poor Brown. Bifty, the master, was having his morning cup of tea in bed and had to get up to stop the row. He was furious and later that day he gave both Billy and Georgie a dreadful beating. Bifty always inspected the floors after a morning scrub and if he had it in for one of us for any reason, out of spite he would make us go back and scrub some part of the floors again.

Breakfast was bread and tea. The bread was already buttered, in that butter had been put on it and scraped off again. There was never enough bread either. During the war butter was rationed at two ounces a week per person, so for 16 boys and the master and his wife and staff there were over two pounds. Bifty in his time took most of this and left for the boys only enough for a scrape for a few days and then nothing at all for the rest of the week.

After breakfast it was school, which was held in a large room on the top floor of the return of the house. There were two big windows that opened outwards on one wall. The floor was bare boards and the master sat beside a turf-burning stove at the top of the room. On his other side there was a blackboard and there was a big map of Ireland on the wall. Each boy sat in an old black single desk with an inkwell. In winter you were cold unless you sat near the front. To the left, in the corner behind the stove, there was a press in which our exercise-books and jotters were kept and *Cúrsaí an Lae,* the only textbook we used apart from the Bible and some English readers. Irish history, Irish geography and arithmetic were taught verbally without textbooks and in addition to learning tables we learned some parts of our other subjects by rote. I had little difficulty learning, but some of the boys were always in trouble.

I have no recollection of an inspector from the Department of Education visiting the school, but during my last three years there we started to learn Irish. I heard later that the Department began to take an interest in homes like the Havergal because they were not teaching Irish and as Protestant establishments they may not have had a commitment to the language. In retrospect it seems that learning Irish was a greater priority for the government than the welfare of orphans.

We didn't have ordinary school exams but we sat the Diocesan Bishop's Medal exam for the whole diocese every year. I enjoyed that exam and usually did well. I won the medal three times but because of the war I never received an actual medal. The prizes for the Diocesan Scripture exams were chits for Bennett's stationery shop beside the Roman Catholic church in O'Connell Street, where there was nothing else to buy except pens, pencils, rubbers and exercise books.

First thing in the morning the subject was Religious Education that was always Bible stories, Old Testament and New. I came to know the Old Testament so well that for me it came alive. I could see the places and I knew the people and lost myself so much in the stories that I felt I was there. I crossed the Red Sea with the Children of Israel, I was there when the walls of Jericho came down, I was on the mountain when Elijah defeated the prophets of Baal and I was in the market place when Amos condemned the injustices of the rich against the poor. These Bible stories, especially from the Old Testament, made me aware of the idea of God taking care of his people. They also gave me a sense of justice and both of these have been with me ever since.

Bifty, when he came, was a particularly good history teacher. He created the scene with word pictures and brought the people alive in my head: Red Hugh O' Neill staking out the bog before the battle of the Yellow Ford, Michael Dwyer with his men hiding in the woods in the Wicklow hills and swooping down to ambush the unsuspecting English soldiers. Bifty wasn't a West

Brit but he wasn't a nationalist either. I don't think it mattered to him what he was so long as he had as comfortable a life as possible, dry turf and plenty of butter.

At one o'clock we had dinner. There was never enough. Cabbage and cabbage water were a great standby: they called the cabbage water soup and after it the slimy cabbage and potatoes. Sometimes there was meat, usually rabbit with either potatoes or vegetables but never both. I was often hungry after I had finished.

After school in the afternoon we were free to play around and stay out of trouble as best we could. This was difficult for young boys in a restricted space. Indoors we hung around the schoolroom reading comics or amusing ourselves. We played marbles and conkers, we made slings or stripped the weeping ash-tree in the garden to make bows and arrows. Outdoors we played a game of our own with a bat and ball against the side wall of the house and we played football at the back. When we hadn't a ball for football we made one with newspapers wrapped up tightly and tied with string. Under the master's supervision the boys did all of the gardening. Before the spring growth we planted daffodils and hyacinths in the flowerbed at the front and after blooming we lifted them and stored the bulbs to dry for the next year's planting. In the garden at the back we grew cabbage, onions and shallots.

Tea was bread and tea again, the same as breakfast, when we got three 'skuds' or slices of loaf each. The families of some of the boys kept in touch with them and the mother of one of these boys, Barrer, used to send him food parcels from time to time. Barrer, who was known as the Cork Cooneyite, would auction some of the food and the only commodity we had to bid with were the skuds we got for tea. At one time I owed Barrer almost all my skuds and I would have to watch while he took them and gave them to his friends. I soon learned not to make those kinds of deals with him or anyone else.

One evening after tea Miss O'Neill, the cook, on her way home found me crying at the back door.

'What's wrong with you?' She asked.

'I'm hungry,' I replied.

'Come with me,' She said, and she took me to Gavin's shop around the corner in Davis Street and bought me three currant buns. Miss O'Neill lived in a little flat near Tate's Clock and worked for a paltry wage. I never forgot that kindness and after I left the Havergal, whenever I was back in Limerick I would go to see her.

Mickey, the master when I first went to the Home, loved crubeens. He had a little pantry under the schoolroom where he boiled them at night and next day he would heat the crubeens and suck them for his lunch. Mickey did not use a cane. He used the leg of a chair that he kept in different hiding places around the house. There was a boy, Cuddy, who was lawless. One day at lunchtime Mickey was sitting in the kitchen sucking his crubeens when Cuddy appeared at the window outside. He had Mickey's chair leg in one hand and a hatchet in the other. He held up the leg of the chair and then the hatchet lest Mickey be in any doubt about what he was going to do. Then he held the chair leg on the ground and began to chop it. By the time Mickey got outside he had disappeared.

Class began at 10 o'clock every weekday and Cuddy was nearly always late. One morning he arrived at about half past ten and Mickey said to him:

'Cuddy, come up here.'

Cuddy went up and stood in front of Mickey at his table beside the stove.

'Why are you late again?'

Cuddy took out a little rubber water squirter and said:

'Would you dare me do this, sir?'

For a terrible moment he stood grinning at Mickey. Then he squirted the master straight in the face and ran. None of us believed he would do it. Neither did Mickey who, after an instant of disbelief, jumped up and chased Cuddy out the door, down the stairs and out into the garden. We all followed like a lot of hunters determined to be in at the kill. The chase around the garden became a mêlée during which I fell to the ground when another boy stood on me and broke my collarbone. This distracted Mickey from the chase and Cuddy escaped for the moment. Cuddy was in trouble so often I cannot remember what his punishment was on this occasion.

Dr Shire, a long straight lady who was the doctor for the home, came in and strapped up my shoulder and said I was to stay in bed for a few days. Mickey sent for Archdeacon Waller and that evening he arrived up in the dormitory where we were all getting ready for bed. Cuddy was there still uncontrollable.

'Come over here, Cuddy,' said the Archdeacon, and instead of going over to the Archdeacon he started to dance around the room and jump from one bed to another beside me.

'Oh the boy's shoulder, the boy's shoulder,' said the Archdeacon. Eventually Mickey and the Archdeacon caught Cuddy, calmed him down and gave him a good talking to. In due course it was decided that Cuddy would have to go to another home, where, we did not know. Somebody brought him down-town and bought him some new clothes. When he came to say goodbye he was dressed in a new suit and was his usual irrepressible self: 'Look,' he said, 'new boots and all.'

Mickey didn't last long after that and Bifty arrived, with his wife, to replace him. The Havergal was a tough place to be and Bifty was as tough as they come. He walked with a peculiar gait, he had duck's disease – he walked with his flat feet at ten-to-two. He told us he had broken both his ankles playing golf and we believed him. Years later I found out he had been a primary schoolteacher in Co Wicklow and lived over the school. The story was that he and another man had been lifting timber from an estate and one night the Guards arrived at the school. He jumped out the upstairs window at the back to escape and broke both his ankles and that was why he walked like a duck. His wife was a decent little woman but she had terrible arthritis, much worse than 'Bummy'. Miss O'Neill the cook used to say Mrs Neely had pains here, and here, and here, pointing to different parts of her body and always ending up with her bottom.

One Sunday after church I was up in the dormitory for something and came out onto the landing. Mrs Neely was on the landing trying to bend down to pick up the enamel cased oil-burner she used to make Bifty his early morning cup of tea. She would carry it downstairs from time to time to trim the wicks and clean it. Since her arthritis made her slow on the stairs I volunteered to carry it.

'I'll carry that down for you, Ma'am,' I said, lifting it off the landing. I went ahead of her down the two flights of stairs and on about the third step from the bottom I tripped and fell. The oil rings crashed onto the stone-flagged floor and the enamel broke in smithereens. I knew I was in trouble. I was terrified. I got up and ran past Mrs Neely up the stairs and hid in a cupboard in the dormitory. I heard Bifty's footsteps on the stairs. I knew what to expect and I wasn't disappointed. The door of the dormitory crashed open. He was fuming and had a stick in his hand. He dragged me out of the cupboard and beat me. He beat me and beat me and beat me. I grabbed him by the legs and pleaded with him to stop but he wouldn't. I broke away from him and crawled under the beds to the far corner of the room, but he pulled the beds aside, dragged me out and beat me more. I thought he would never stop and I carried the marks of that beating on my back for months. I showed them to Miss O'Neill who told me I should go to the Guards. That was the terrible thing about it – there was no appeal. It was the terrible thing about orphanages in those days where children were abused in one way or another; you were trapped, there was no way out. There was no appeal.

Children can be cruel to each other too and the boys of the Havergal were no exception. There were fights, of course, from time to time, but when they were finished they were over and done with. The physical cruelty was not the worst. A new boy arrived in the home whose face had the look of a primate. One of the others, who was no oil painting himself, began a long story about how he had read in the paper that a chimpanzee had escaped from the zoo in Dublin and someone had seen it getting off the train in Limerick. This continued in the dormitory at night with others chipping in to elaborate the story to the complete demolition of the new arrival. Ever after he was known as 'Chimp'.

Bifty used to come into the dormitory every night to be sure we were all there and to put out the light. I had no access to a radio and I used to ask him about the war and he'd give us a progress report. I have a clear memory of the war being over and in due course he gave us accounts of the Nuremberg trials and how Goering committed suicide and some of the others were hanged.

The Archdeacon came into the home once or twice a week and if there was anything of note to tell us, or if there was a serious matter of discipline, he would address us all together. On one occasion in Mickey's time there had been horseplay that went too far. The next time the Archdeacon was in, Mickey gave him an account of the fights that had ensued. He called four of us out, stood us in a line and sent Mickey for a cane. The only thing Mickey had was the chair leg that, predictably, he didn't bring to the Archdeacon, but he came back with a stick from somewhere. The Archdeacon looked at the stick with some reservation and told us to hold out our hands. I was first.

'This will hurt me more than it will hurt you,' he said and laid the stick gently on my hand and lifted it off again. His tactic worked. I felt much worse than if he had given me five of the best. I felt so small and ashamed; I wanted to crawl into a corner. I felt for the old boy, and despite his stature and status I was fond of him. I knew he cared for the boys in a distant kind of way and wanted to do the best for us according to his own values.

The boys of the Havergal were *ex officio* members of the 1st Limerick scout troop attached to the parish. The assistant scoutmaster was Mr Montgomery who was, in fact, English but he had a high regard for his adopted country and Irish republicanism. From him I got my first feel for being Irish. He told me that despite the fact that his people were from England they had been in Ireland all through the War of Independence, and the reason he gave his loyalty to the country was that he and his family carried on with their lives during that time in the normal way without any interference whatever. He felt he owed his loyalty to a country that would do this in the circumstances. He talked to me about the concept of true republicanism and I took in a lot from him.

We went to scouts one night a week at the Diocesan Hall and did the usual things. We learned to tie knots, worked for badges and learned to light fires without matches. I was a member of the curlew patrol. The annual camps were exciting for us – living in tents, cooking food, good food, and doing chores – all a great breath of fresh air in every sense. Then there were outings and games and campfires at night. One year there was a scout jamboree in Cratloe Woods and the new chief scout, Lord Rowallan, was due to arrive. There was great excitement and everything had to be spick and span. When he arrived at our tent we saluted and he inspected the tent and our uniforms and shook hands – the boys of the Havergal shaking hands with a real live Lord!

On bank holidays it was one of the duties of the curate of the parish to take us all out for long hikes in the country. I hated them. On one of these hikes I told the curate, the Rev George Kingston, all about how little food we got and about Bifty and the butter and the cabbage water and how we were always hungry. He asked me questions and I wasn't backward in making my case. The curate lived in a house owned by Dr Shire, who was a returned medical missionary and a very religious woman. He told her what I had told him about the food and Dr Shire told the Archdeacon.

On 1st April, (the date is etched in my memory) the Archdeacon came into the home in a dreadful temper and stood up in front of the whole school. He was white and shaking with anger and we knew something terrible was coming. He fumed about people talking outside and running down the Havergal. He told us how difficult it was in hard times to keep the place going on voluntary contributions, something we knew nothing at all about. All we knew was that much of the time we were hungry. Then he rounded on me by name, pointing me out and abusing me for what I had told the curate about the food:

'You,' he said, 'whose people, if you had any people, never gave a brass farthing to this home. You, with nobody belonging to you who ever gave a penny to your keep here, how dare you run down this home to others. Have you no gratitude for what we have done for you that you run down this home that has given you shelter since you came here when you had nowhere else to go and when nobody else wanted you.'

It was awful and I was devastated. It didn't seem to matter to the Archdeacon that what I had said to the curate just might have been true. He didn't want to know that what he regarded as part of his life's work might have had flaws. I was desolate. In a place like the Havergal you had to try to keep some self-worth and you grasped at every rare hint of affirmation. He may not have realised it but he almost annihilated me. I cried and cried on and off for days. For years afterwards I remembered that humiliating tongue-lashing, and every April the 1st it still comes back to me.

The Archdeacon came from an aristocratic family. One of his forebears sat at the trial of Charles I when he was sentenced to death and another forebear, a member of the Irish Parliament, voted against the Act of Union. His was a background of money and privilege. He was a good man, kind in his own way, but he was strong and dominant, with a ferocious temper, and he couldn't brook criticism. Despite his Christianity criticism of the food in the Havergal, that he must have known to be true, could elicit a devastating attack on a defenceless young boy. It was far and away a worse experience for me than any beating I had. I blamed the curate for it and I couldn't bring myself to speak to him for ages. When we met I would give him an unfriendly side-long glance and move away. Eventually we made it up when he gave me a shilling. To blame the curate of course was unfair of me since I did hope that by telling him he could somehow do something about the food. I thought perhaps he would go to Bifty. It never occurred to me it would get to the Archdeacon.

The Archdeacon came in every week to talk to us. One morning he came in, not on his usual day, and he was quite excited. He told us that Princess Elizabeth had had a son, a new prince had been born. He sometimes spoke about the British Empire and on one occasion he told us about a man who was chased by natives somewhere in Africa. He said this man was in danger of his life and some of his friends caught him and wrapped the Union Jack around him and told the natives that if they touched him now they'd be taking on the whole British Empire. This didn't really make much of an impression on me, for my chats with the assistant scoutmaster had nurtured an incipient republicanism that has never left me.

Not only were we hungry but during the winter we were cold. On cold days we would 'bag' places near the fire to get a heat. The deliveries of turf were often wet and hard to burn. There is great heat from a good turf fire but when the turf is wet there is smoke and no heat. Bifty kept all the dry turf for himself and when a dry load was delivered he stored it separately under lock and key. One day a couple of us were filling buckets of turf for the schoolroom.

'That stuff over there, boy.' He was a great man for calling us 'boy'.

'It's all wet,' I said. 'How are we going to light the fire with it?'

'You can take two sods of the dry stuff.'

'You never give us enough dry turf, you keep it all for yourself,' I said, 'and leave us with only wet turf. It's not fair, we're always cold. I'm going to tell the Archdeacon.'

From then on he gave us much more of the dry turf!

We had a bath once a week. They lit the fire in the bathroom and heated the water in a big black pot over the fire. The smoke from the damp turf filled the bathroom and made our eyes run. There was great competition to be first into the clean hot water. Five or six boys used the same water, which was cold and filthy before it was changed for the next lot.

A boy in the Havergal could not but be conscious that he was the object of charity. As with Miss Carr's Home, parishes gave vegetables and fruit from Harvest Thanksgiving Services to the home. Wesley College in Dublin used to send down old rugby jerseys when they were past use for us to use as everyday wear. I hated those blue shirts with white collars because I knew they were other people's casts off. They marked us out, as it were, like wearing a uniform. When we needed a haircut we were sent to a barber around the corner in Davis Street who had instructions to shave our heads to short stubble that made us look like convicts. We were impatient for it to grow again. On the morning of one parish children's party in the Diocesan Hall Bifty sent me to get my hair cut and I refused to go to the party in the afternoon. I have no doubt that Bifty did it on purpose that day to get his own back for one of the times I stood up to him. At the party the Archdeacon asked where I was and he sent Bifty back to get me. Of course I had to go but I had registered my protest about the haircuts.

Apart from Christmas it was rare for any of us to have money. Occasionally a member of the family of one of the boys might visit and give them sixpence or even a shilling. One evening when we were in the schoolroom doing lessons, Gerry Wooster had some money and was determined he was going out to buy sweets. He got out the schoolroom window, which was on the second floor, and climbed down the drainpipe into the garden and out over the ten-foot wall. When he had gone I closed the window and I was waiting inside when he got back. He tried the window and couldn't open it.

'Dalton, open the window.'

'I will if you give me some sweets.'

'Dalton, I'm telling you if you don't open the window I'll break it.'

'Go ahead,' said I, in the hope that he'd give me sweets to let him in.

He put his fist through the window and when I saw it was covered in blood I started to cry and opened the window. Bifty arrived and we were both in trouble again.

We were allowed out of the home with permission if there was good reason. Conway's Hackney Service was almost opposite the Havergal. One of the children of this family died. Late that night in the dormitory we woke up terrified to the sound of screeching. It was the grandmother of the family sitting in the middle of Lord Edward Street, keening. None of us had ever heard keening before and didn't know what was going on. Next day a few of us decided to go over to the house to offer our condolences. We were shown into the parlour where the little girl was in the coffin in the middle of the room and people were saying the rosary and crying. All the appurtenances of Catholicism, that weren't part of our tradition, were there: a crucifix, lighted candles, rosary beads, statues and holy pictures. Two shawlies were kneeling beside the coffin praying and we didn't know what to do, so we walked slowly and reverently around the coffin looking at the little corpse, then we stood quietly for a minute and without a word we shook hands with the mother and left. I sensed a particular friendliness from the Conways for the boys of the Havergal after that.

The Archdeacon gave us the job of delivering the parish magazine, which was a great excuse to get out for an afternoon. We went all over the city and as far as the Ennis Road. The parishioners knew us as the orphans from the home. Most of them were friendly towards us and the odd one would give us a sweet or a biscuit.

If we had money we would slip out unknown to the master and go up to Naughton's chip shop on Parnell Street. For two pence we got a bag of chips that assuaged the hunger, and they were tastier than any of the food we got in the home. On Saturday afternoons, again if we had money, we went to the matinee at one of the cinemas. We went to the pit, the cheapest seats that were wooden benches at the front where you would get a crick in your neck looking up at the screen. In the Lyric, however, the cheapest seats were up in the gods. The noise and pushing and shoving and sometimes the fights before the picture started were intimidating to us. You had to be careful as anything might happen. If you were distracted someone might even pee in your pocket. If the film turned out to be boring, just for diversion boys would throw missiles of anything they had up into the light that projected the film onto the screen, and a kiss on screen was inevitably accompanied by a loud roar from the pit.

Gene Autrey and Roy Rogers cowboy films were our favourites, when the star always won in the end. For a couple of hours we were absorbed in the fantasy. Then out of the cinema and back to reality where boys extended the fantasy by running through pedestrians on the busy street, ducking into doorways and shooting at each other with two fingers and making the sound of gunfire. One afternoon at the pictures a man sitting beside me tried to open my fly. I moved away and fortunately he didn't follow me. I was wary in future not to sit beside a man on his own if I could avoid it.

If a few of us from the home were walking along the street and saw a Roman Catholic priest coming we would space ourselves into single file and each would tip his forehead to him and then giggle at the good of him trying to return each boy's salute. The other kids in the area near the home knew that we were from the Protestant orphanage, and if they saw us coming they used to hide behind the air-raid shelter on Reeves Path and jump out and shout after us:

'Proddy woddy ring the bell, all the soupers go to hell.' And we would shout back:

'Catholic, Catholic go to mass riding on the divil's ass.' Then they'd shout:

'Protestant, Protestant, quack quack quack, go to the divil and never come back.'

The one thing you could say about the Havergal was there was no shortage of religion. Religion was an important part of Miss Carr's Home too and when I was in the Havergal I carried out faithfully Miss Carr's parting instructions to me to say my prayers and read my Bible every day. I found them a reassurance and the more I read about the Children of Israel in the old Testament and how God looked after them, the more I felt I couldn't see any reason why he wouldn't look after me too.

The parish and clergy figured large in our lives. We felt conscious of being connected to the parish but in a sense, since we were from the Havergal, we were not of the parish. We were at one remove and when I met some of the people we saw in church out on the street during the week I felt somehow different from them. One day outside I met a man from the parish who smiled at me and said 'hello'. It made me feel good.

We went to Trinity Church every Sunday morning dressed in our best. We went first to Sunday school with the rest of the children from the parish where Miss Whately and Miss Ewing were the teachers. They seemed to me to be particularly religious women who taught us from the Bible. Then we went to the morning service where we sat in the gallery and supported the choir with the singing. We went again on Sunday evening and we were brought to church at any excuse, Lent, Advent, Christmas, Saints' days, holy days and holidays. On Sunday mornings the Archdeacon's wife watched to see who was not in church. She sat half way up the church and during the creed she turned her head eyeing the whole congregation, and even while she bowed her head saying 'I believe in Jesus Christ,' her head kept moving on as she noted vacant pews, until she had covered the whole church. That evening at the rectory after supper, we learned from the curate, her husband would ask her, 'Well Ali who was missing this morning?' On Monday the Archdeacon, complete with gaiters, would mount his bicycle and visit anyone who wasn't out on Sunday, presumably on the pretext that they might have been unwell, at the same time putting them on notice if they weren't.

In the Diocesan Hall on Tuesday afternoons the Archdeacon and his wife taught us choruses and hymns. Mrs Waller was from the North of Ireland. She was a tall dignified and lady-like figure who told us how much she liked the 'Hallelujah chorus', it was so triumphant. I assume her name was Alice or Alison, since the Archdeacon always called her 'Ali'. She played the piano daintily while we sang 'Heavenly Sunshine' and 'There is a Happy Land Far Far Away.' Another I remember well, we called 'the choo, choo chorus':

We're going up to heaven on the happy day express,
The letters on the engine are J E S U S,
The guard cries 'All for heaven?'
We gladly answer 'Yes.'
We're going up to heaven on the happy day express.

Half way through the verse one of the boys at the back would let out a 'whoowhoo, choochoochoochoo'. The Archdeacon would get upset and say to his wife, 'Ali what will I do with them? We'll sing "Heavenly Sunshine" and I'll look away,' and he'd turn sideways and shield his eyes with his hand.

There were two other choruses we sang: 'By and by we'll see the King,' and :

I am H A P P Y, I am H A P P Y,
I know I am, I'm sure I am,
I'm H A P P Y.

Many of the choruses and hymns we learned were about going to heaven and what a grand time we'd have there. Of course we weren't a bit interested in going to heaven. There was genuine concern for our immortal souls and part of the objective of those who ran homes like the Havergal was to save souls. We all had to join the Band of Hope and promised '…with God's help to abstain from all intoxicating liquor as a beverage'. We had cards and badges to mark our membership, and so formal was the making of the promise that I knew it was important. I didn't break that pledge until I was 21, when I was in Dublin and went on a parish youth club outing to Guinness's brewery.

They promoted salvation by appeal to our emotions rather than by rules or regulations. There was religious discipline too of course, like prayers, Bible reading and going to church, but the appeal to the heart was seen as the important thing. If they didn't win over the heart what went in through the head might be wasted.

An opportunity to earn a shilling came in the spring when the Archdeacon brought us all down to St John's Church in the old part of Limerick to clean up the graveyard. It was hard work to cut back the previous summer's growth of briars, nettles and weeds and we earned our shilling. The church was beside St John's Roman Catholic Cathedral with its beautiful slender spire. One day the Archdeacon said to me,

'Kevin, I want to show you something.'

He put his arm around my shoulder and said:

'I want you to look up to the top of that spire. Do you see it? Do you see the fly on the very tip? Have a good look.' And he went on like that for ages. Eventually I said :

'I think I can.'

'Are you sure?'

'Oh yes,' I said.' I can see it.'

'My goodness, Kevin,' he said 'you've great eyesight.'

During my first summer at the Havergal we went to stay for a week by the sea at Clar Ellagh, the Christian Endeavour house in Kilkee. Christian Endeavour was an evangelical organisation and one of their activities was to provide holidays in a Christian atmosphere. There were prayers every morning and every evening.

One afternoon on the beach I was close to some of the Conway family from across the road from the Havergal, where some of us had gone to the wake when the little girl died. I edged my way across the sand until sitting very close to one of the young mothers. I looked up at her and said:

'Don't you love me?'

There was a moment's hesitation while she took in what had I said and then she laughed and her friend beside her laughed with her. I blushed and sidled away as fast and as unobtrusively as I could, hoping that nobody else had heard.

We had a good time on that holiday in Kilkee. At the end of the holiday we were due to return to Limerick on the Friday train, one of two wartime West Clare weekly trains to Limerick. We all wanted to stay longer so we had a secret meeting. Gerry Wooster, the one who went down the drainpipe for the sweets, and who was up to anything, got the job. He could move around like a cat and he got up in the middle of the night and put all the clocks back, not that there were many. Next morning we were lying in bed wide awake, knowing we were going to miss the train, when consternation broke out. The helper got us up immediately. We had a hurried breakfast and made for the station. It was soon clear we wouldn't make the train and we would have to wait until the next one on Monday. Over the weekend we were in makeshift accommodation. We were all in disgrace and severely restricted in our movements over the weekend.

When we got back to the Havergal the Archdeacon arrived into the home to give us one of his lectures. He was in one of his foul tempers and devoured us. What did we think we were doing? Had we no gratitude? Later on in the summer we were due to go to camp with the scouts so as a punishment he would not let us go. We were left hanging around the orphanage for the rest of the summer holiday with nothing to do.

Living in the Havergal provided me with food, clothing and shelter. It provided school and the order and shape to the day but it didn't provide the emotional security that every human being needs. It did however provide the religious teaching, especially of the Old Testament, teaching about a God who looked after his people if they were faithful to him. This sense of a God who would look after me grew slowly and steadily during my time in Limerick and gave me confidence that I would be all right in the future – but how, I did not know.

Later that year a significant event for me occurred. The Kemmis's, to whose home in Co Wicklow we had been evacuated during the war, had kept in touch with Miss Carr after we left Ballinacor. Mrs Kemmis supported the home and sent £5 every year for pound day. In one of her letters Miss Carr told Mrs Kemmis that I was in Limerick, so she wrote to the Archdeacon and arranged for me to spend Christmas with her and the Captain at their other estate, Moyaliffe, near Thurles in Co Tipperary.

Mrs Kemmis was one of three sisters whose only brother had been killed in the First World War. She inherited Moyaliffe which had been her home before she was married and she and the Captain lived between Moyaliffe, and his family home,

Ballinacor, and ran both of them as working farms. During the days before the holidays I was both excited and apprehensive. I was excited because I wouldn't have to spend Christmas in the home, and I looked forward to seeing the dogs, Barney and Chips, and Mopsy the rabbit, but I was apprehensive not knowing what lay ahead. I remembered my time at Ballinacor with the rest of the children from Miss Carr's Home but I didn't know what to expect at Moyaliffe and I wondered would I be left on my own. Roughly half the boys in the Havergal were orphans and stayed there for Christmas and the other half had families, such as they were, to go to.

CHAPTER THREE

Another World

It was 1942 and as the time came closer for my first Christmas holiday my excitement increased, and although apprehension diminished, it did not disappear altogether. Like some of the boys who had families of their own I would not be spending Christmas in the Havergal and that in itself was something to be excited about.

The day arrived, and Bifty put me on the bus in Limerick with instructions to the conductor to let this ten-year-old boy off in Rosmult. I had never been on a bus before and I had no idea how long the journey would take. It seemed endless and it was punctuated by stops for people to get on and off in towns and villages whose names I did not know, and sometimes in total darkness in the middle of nowhere. Eventually the conductor called me as the bus slowed for another stop to tell me it was Rosmult. When I got off the bus a man approached me and knew my name. He brought me over to a horse and cart and lifted me up and I sat at the front on the opposite side of the horse to him. It was dark and I had no idea how far it was to Moyaliffe. It was cold on the cart as we trundled through the darkness further into the country. I could see the outline of hedgerows on either side and remembered ghost stories that some of the boys told in the dormitory at night. The countryside was quiet apart from the noise of the steel-rimmed wheels on the stony road and the breathing and occasional snort of the horse.

Early in the journey the man asked me a couple of questions and then lapsed into silence. The journey seemed to go on for ever. The further we went the more frightened I became and the more certain I was that he was kidnapping me. I thought of jumping off the cart and running, but in the black darkness in the middle of the country I might never be heard of again.

Eventually we came to a crossroads near a small village and then crossed over a bridge when the man pointed across the fields to lights in the distance and said: 'That's where we're going.' I still wasn't sure. It was another twenty or twenty-five minutes before we came to a pair of large gates, open, and a gate-lodge, leading to an avenue lined on both sides with bare wintry trees that formed an arch overhead.

Then a large house, lit up, came into view. It was a magical sight and the wonder of it is still with me. The man drove to the corner of the house, lifted me down with my bag, brought me to the hall-door and rang the bell. Through the glass in the door I could see Barney and Chips bounding down the wide oak-panelled hall lined with the heads of animals, hunting trophies from exotic parts of the world. Captain and Mrs Kemmis came after them and brought me in. They made a great fuss and said how much they had been looking forward to seeing me again. I was excited and happy.

They brought me down a long stone passage at the back of the house to the kitchen and introduced me to Flannery the chef, O'Connor the butler and Miss Doran the housekeeper. I knew what a housekeeper was but I had never come across a chef or a butler before. They were all very friendly and told me how welcome I was. Nobody had ever said that to me before. For them it must have been a novelty to have a child in the house. Then my host and hostess took me up to a small room at the back where they sat with me while I had something to eat. When I finished Mrs Kemmis took me upstairs for a hipbath and then to the bedroom beside the Captain's dressing-room where I was to sleep. Mrs Kemmis sat with me while I said my prayers and got into bed. When she left I lay in the dark in total silence in this big old house in the middle of Co Tipperary not knowing what lay ahead.

Next morning a maid came in and said 'Good Morning,' and put a copper carrier of hot water beside the ewer on the washstand. Without a word she opened the curtains and the sunlight streamed into the room, giving me a different perspective on my surroundings from the one I had had the night before. When the maid left I got up, went to the window and looked out onto a long lawn with fields beyond stretching into the distance. The only sound was the ripple of a small river running past to the left of the lawn. The only movement was the gentle swaying of the treetops in a grove to the right. I stood looking until I began to feel cold and then I poured the water into the bowl and washed. It was the first time I had ever had a morning wash with warm water.

After a while the Captain arrived to take me downstairs for breakfast. There was a pervasive smell of mustiness. Around the three-sided landing there were other bedrooms and at the bottom of the stairs in the hall the uniform and medals of Mrs Kemmis's brother, who had been killed in the First War, were displayed in a glass case on the wall above his portrait. To the right there was a large drawing room with French windows that opened out onto well-tended lawns with rose beds and six yew trees. Double doors led into the morning-room at the front of the house. To the left the dining-room with the longest table I had ever seen and on the sideboard at one end of the room there was a huge display of silver. Men of solemn countenance and one or two women looked down from the walls on the Captain at one end of the table and Mrs Kemmis at the other and at myself sitting like a lord on Mrs Kemmis's right. I learned later that there was a family tradition that when the head of the family was about to die one in particular of these portraits was said to fall off the wall and end up in the fireplace. Everything was a fascination to me, but the greatest fascination of all was to have a maid in cap and apron serving me my breakfast.

After breakfast the Captain brought me outside to show me around. From the far end of the lawn I looked back. The house was two-storeyed, rambling and of great character. The main house had two windows on either side of a gabled porch. There was a return with a wing. All the wall surfaces were covered with ivy, trimmed around the windows. The small river, with clumps of bamboo on the near bank, flowed along the right-hand side of the lawn and past the music room and the engine house where electricity was generated for the house. The house stood against a backdrop of mature trees, mainly oak and beech amongst which laurel grew. These trees and laurel were grow-ing on a large hillock under which was the ruin of the old castle, the original dwelling, the stone staircase of which protruded above the laurels.

The Captain brought me around the back of the house past the walled garden to the stable yard, introduced me to Plunkett, the steward, and left. I then went exploring the yards and the big walled garden and talked to staff and workmen that I met. I was curious to know what they were doing and most of them took time to tell me. They were all friendly and polite and in some cases almost deferential. I had no sense that they were what the Captain and Mrs Kemmis called servants. When Mrs Kemmis discovered that I had been talking to the men she told me that when talking to the servants I must always refer to the Captain as 'the Master' and to her as 'the Mistress'.

I explored the laurel walks and the grove of mature trees at the side of the lawn where I discovered small headstones in-scribed with the names of family dogs. They reminded me of the funerals for birds and kittens we held in the back garden of Miss Carr's Home when we marked the grave with a stick that didn't survive for very long. I walked the bank of the river at the back of the house and came to a bathhouse where members of the family in the past used to change to swim in a pool in the river.

I came to know all of the staff, outside and inside and with-out exception they accepted me warmly and looked after me. During that holiday I spent a good deal of my time with Ned Burke whose main work was with the cows. I begged him to let me try to milk, and eventually he gave in and taught me. Inside, the butler John O'Connor became a good friend. Flannery, the chef, was from Galway; he was a most agreeable man with a friendly smile. Miss Doran, the housekeeper, whose room was upstairs beside the Captain and Mrs Kemmis's bedroom, was elderly. She dressed entirely in black and never smiled. I found her forbidding; in fact at first I was afraid of her. There were two bookcases of books in her room and these were a great attraction for me. Mrs Kemmis allowed me to take these books to my room to read. On this and on future visits I read many of them, especially children's classics, *Treasure Island, Black Beauty, The Scarlet Pimpernel, The Three Musketeers, Robinson Crusoe, King Solomon's Mines* and most of Dickens. This was where I learned to enjoy reading and that added greatly to my time at Moyaliffe. There was one book, *The Rat Pit*, by Patrick MacGill, about emigration from Donegal to Scotland, that I found disturbing and sad. It is a story I have never forgotten.

I ate my meals with Captain and Mrs Kemmis in the diningroom and sat with them sometimes in the drawing-room and read. Sometimes I was allowed to stay in the smoking-room on my own and listen to the wireless. In the gun room one wall was covered with maps and every day the Captain would mark with little arrows the advance or retreat of the Allied armies. He would bring me into the room with him as he plotted the progress of the war on his maps, and explain to me the most recent news. Occasionally I went out in the car with the Captain to Thurles or to call on somebody nearby. However, I spent most of my time out in the yard or the garden or out in the fields with the men tending stock. The Havergal was a million miles away.

For Christmas there were decorations in the hall. Heavily berried holly decorated the tops of picture frames and holly was to be found in the most unlikely places around the house. On Christmas morning I went to church at Holy Cross with Captain and Mrs Kemmis. When we arrived back from church, before lunch, Mrs Kemmis had two boxes full of presents waiting for me, all of them wrapped in Christmas paper and tied with coloured ribbon. As I began to open them there were so many I wondered would I ever get to the end of them. I had never had such a Christmas and, being the only child in the house, I received a great deal of attention.

A few days before I was due to return to the Havergal early in the New Year, an incident occurred that may well have been a momentous event in my life. During the night I woke with cramps in my stomach and badly needed to go to the lavatory. I was disinclined in the black darkness to cross the landing to the bathroom a distance away, so I used the pot under my bed. After all, wasn't that what it was for? I got back into bed and fell fast asleep. Next morning I heard the Captain coming down the passageway towards my bedroom saying, 'Oh Jess, the smell is dreadful, it's dreadful.' I believe that it was as a result of this that on my next visit to Moyaliffe I was moved to the servants' quarters. In fact I was more relaxed out with the staff and I enjoyed the banter and the fun. It was more in my line than the formal atmosphere of the house.

My first Christmas holiday at Moyaliffe was the best of my life and as the day approached to return to Limerick something of a state of melancholy descended upon me. I tried not to think about it but inexorably the day arrived. I packed my few things into my bag and took with me the Christmas presents I had been given. I went around to say goodbye to all the staff, some of whom said things like 'We'll see you again.' This gave me some hope, but did not lift my dampened spirits. At the door, while Marty waited outside with the horse and cart to take me to the bus, Captain and Mrs Kemmis said goodbye and something non-committal about coming again. As the horse picked up speed going down the avenue I could not hold back the tears any longer and I cried on and off from there to the bus. As I approached Limerick I had a heavy heart as I contemplated Bifty and the other boys and the routine of the Havergal, but this time at least I had a story to tell.

The entry in Mrs Kemmis's diary for that day said: 'Poor little Kevin goes back to school today.'

CHAPTER FOUR

Moyaliffe

Over the next seven years I spent most of my Easter, summer and Christmas holidays at Moyaliffe. It made life at the Havergal bearable to know that at the end of term I would be returning to the idyllic surroundings of the estate and farm that I came to love. Now that I lived in the servants' quarters I was as happy as Larry and completely at ease. I came to know all the staff well and they looked after me. A great bonus was the good wholesome food – plenty of brown bread and country butter, eggs, milk galore, meat, potatoes and vegetables. I was never hungry when I was in Moyaliffe. During the day I spent my time with the workmen at their jobs in the yard or on the land or in the walled garden with the gardeners. I could pick and choose what I would do – I was a free agent.

Mrs Kemmis, more so than the Captain, was the one who kept a close eye on the staff and kept them on their toes. They never knew when or where she would turn up. After all, Moyaliffe was her home. Her father had entrusted it to her rather than to either of her sisters, after her brother's death in the war, because he knew she loved the place. She was sometimes a bit of a tyrant with the staff and when she became angry she could be belligerent, but the staff took it from her no matter what she said to them. I was never quite sure if that was pure subservience or whether they just allowed for her ways.

Moyaliffe Estate was a farm of about 600 acres of mostly arable land. Every morning at eight o'clock Ned Burke rang the bell in the little belfry at the entrance to the farmyard, to signal the start of the day's work. The men gathered in the stable before eight and sat on the straw to wait for the bell and to receive their orders from the steward for their day's work. There were, of course, some jobs that were done every day. I usually went off with Ned to milk the cows. We brought them into the cowshed with the help of Silvo the dog, chained them up to the stall and milked them sitting on three-legged stools. We then carried the milk to the dairy in buckets and poured it through a large muslin sieve into big circular flat pans about two inches deep. It sat there until the cream settled on top, and Kate or Nora from the kitchen skimmed it off to churn butter for the house. When we had delivered the milk to the dairy Ned and I would go back to the farmyard and, again with Silvo's help, drive the cows out to the field. Then we would go back to the cow house, clean it out, and make new straw bedding for the next milking.

During the Easter holidays there was usually ploughing, tilling or sowing, all with horses. I helped to harness the horses and yoke them into plough, harrow or sower for the day's work. I would run along beside the workman ploughing and for a little while he would let me take the reins on the long straight runs of a big field.

The Christmas holidays were short and apart from milking, foddering cattle and feeding hens and geese there was little else to do. There were always two or three geese and a gander at Moyaliffe and when I was there I used to look after them. They were in an enclosed space in the yard and I brought their food in a bucket and dished it out over the low gate with a long handled metal spoon. Sometimes the gander, who was always aggressive, would grip the spoon in his beak, and I would lean over the gate, catch him by the neck, swing him round and round and let him go. He would fly away a few yards, and turning as he landed he would race back, squawking, with his neck stretched out to attack again.

I was particularly fond of Marty Gleeson and went with him to the fields to fodder the cattle most days. He was the one I thought was kidnapping me when he collected me from the bus on my first visit to Moyaliffe. I used to sit up on the cart beside him and when the horse broke wind Marty would turn to me and say: 'You're a dirty young fella'.'

One day on the way back from foddering the cattle in the fields, as we crossed the avenue towards the paddock, Marty asked me to get down and open the gate.

'No,' I said 'I'm going to drive the horse.'

'You're not,' he said. 'Get down and open the gate.'

'I will not.' And I stayed where I was and folded my arms.

Marty relented and said 'All right, but be careful.'

As soon as he got down and opened the gate I hit the horse a crack with the stick and he took off, leaving Marty standing. The horse began to gallop and I began to get frightened. I pulled on the reins and shouted at the horse, but to no avail. By now I was really frightened and beat the horse with the stick to get him to stop. This of course made him worse. I was hopping up and down holding on as best I could when I saw the sharp right hand bend towards the yard ahead. I knew we wouldn't make it, so I edged onto the shaft and with both my hands I shot myself forward onto the ground and rolled away as fast as I could. The cart turned over and hit the ground behind me pulling the horse down. Fortunately he was not injured and neither was I, though I was badly shaken. Marty arrived on the scene none too pleased with my performance and while I was determined to let him see I wasn't hurt, I made him promise never to tell the Captain or Mrs Kemmis.

Johnny McGlynn used to drive the horses to town to collect goods for the farm and the house, and I would often go with him. He was always sure to visit a pub and of course he would buy lemonade for me. Johnny and I got on well; he was great fun. He lived in a thatched cottage at the foot of Moyaliffe Hill with Molly, his wife, who was much older than him and they had three grown up children. I loved to visit them at night and sit by the open fire, turn the bellows and listen to the chat. Sometimes they would play the gramophone – usually John McCormack or cowboy songs.

Johnny's father and grandfather had worked on the estate and he himself had worked there all his life. He was supposed to have been involved with the IRA during the Troubles when they tried to burn down Moyaliffe. After 1922, when all was quiet again, one day Mrs Kemmis asked Johnny:

'How could you have been involved with trying to burn down Moyaliffe?'

'Ah, Madam,' he said, 'I was distracted over poor Master Marcus. I was so upset I didn't know what I was doing.' Master Marcus, Mrs Kemmis's brother, was killed in action in 1918!

If I associate Limerick with rain I associate Moyaliffe with sun and warmth. It was an ideal place for a young boy to spend the long summer holiday and one of the highlights of the summer was making hay. The key to good hay is fine weather at haymaking – 'make hay while the sun shines.' In those days there was a horse-drawn mowing-machine for cutting the meadow. The cut grass was left to dry and turned a number of times until it was dry enough to be gathered into ridges by a horse and rake, then it was forked into small mounds, later to be built into stacks. The experienced man could gather in stray pieces to make a forkful of just the right size to build a small mound so that it would lie loose enough to allow the air through it to go on drying the hay, and not too loose that it might be damaged by wind. When the hay was ready and the weather was fine all the men on the place were put to stacking hay. It was hard work on a hot day and it was more skilful than it appeared to an inexperienced youngster like myself.

It was my job to go back to the kitchen and bring a basket of tea and sandwiches to the field for the men when they would sit against a haystack away from the sun to take their break. I listened to the conversation of local news and gossip and of girls and dancing and talk of hurling, which I had come to know a little about from going to matches in Thurles with the men. When a number of workmen were together, being the youngest and the greenest in the ways of the world, I had constantly to be on my guard against some trick or joke at my expense. When the hay was ready to be brought in, one of the men backed a horse-drawn hay float under the cocks and brought them into the hayshed to be stored for winter feed. At the end of July if the hay was all in and if Tipperary had beaten Cork in the Munster hurling final, you would hear the men say with great satisfaction: 'The hay saved and Cork bet.'

Sometimes I spent the day in the garden where Mr Henn was the head gardener. He was the only Protestant who worked on the estate and had been there since Mrs Kemmis was a girl. He had some kind of back problem and was bent double with his back parallel to the ground, and he had a huge nose. He was the only person on the place that Mrs Kemmis never patronised. She had known him all her life and she trusted him completely. Whenever Mrs Kemmis came out to talk to him he always ended their conversation with:

'Well you know, Madam, I'm so busy I never have a minute for to call my own.'

Kate Healy, the cook, disliked Henn intensely. When the fruit was ready for picking Mr Henn would go to Mrs Kemmis rather than tell Kate, and he wouldn't let her into the garden except to pick fruit. She always referred to him as 'the old hen'.

Jimmy Fitzgerald was the under-gardener. He used to do the digging and heavy work and drive the wheelbarrow. Jimmy used to romance about trees and plants and talk about all kinds of things that were harmless but irrelevant to the rest of us. Norah McGlynn, one of the housemaids, used to say that Jimmy had 'holy purity'. I was never sure what 'holy purity' was. As far as I was concerned he had a bit of a lack, but I liked him.

When the fruit was ripe I used to help to pick the black, red and white currants, the raspberries, strawberries and gooseberries, and I would eat my fill while I was at it. I had to top and tail the currants and the gooseberries, a job I did not care for. The apples and pears weren't ripe until after I had gone back to Limerick, but this didn't stop me sampling them to find out.

I did have a couple of routine jobs to do. The pleasant one, unless it was raining, was to bring the postbag to Brennan's in the afternoon. The postbag was a black leather pouch that folded over on itself, and clipped into small hoops on the front. To close it a metal rod was passed through the hoops and secured with a lock. The Captain and the Post Office both had keys. In the afternoon I brought it down the front lawn, across the fields, past the old graveyard, over the coffin-stile and down the road to Brennan's to where the postman collected it. Next morning he brought the bag back, locked by the Post Office, containing the days post along with *The Irish Times*.

The two Misses Brennan were aunts of Ned Burke's who lived with them. They both dressed in black and wore aprons of sacking tied at the back with binder twine. The kitchen was inside the half-door on the right. On one wall there was a large dresser with plates propped up on the shelves and mugs hanging on hooks under them. A flitch of home-cured bacon might hang from one of the hooks in the ceiling and a white enamel pail of spring water, covered with a board, stood on a chair in the corner. Beside it there was a small milk churn on another chair. The walls of the kitchen were whitewashed and on one wall there was a picture of the sacred heart with a small oil lamp burning beneath it. Beside it there was a picture of Pope Pius XII. The floor was made of stone flags and the fire beneath the open chimney, with the bellows that I loved to turn, was the very heart of the kitchen. Above the fire were the fire irons with black kettle and pots, and if bread was baking in one of the pots hot coals were placed on the lid.

From time to time I passed the time with the country sports normally associated with a large estate like Moyaliffe – hunting shooting and fishing! I used to ride Redeye, my favourite horse barebacked around the yard and out into the fields. Redeye was a big gentle horse, too quiet to get me into any trouble. I loved him.

In the yard there was a hut on wheels where the mash for the hens was kept in barrels. Rats got into these barrels and as the level of feed went down the rats couldn't get out, and my hunting consisted of lifting Silvo up by the scruff and the tail and putting him into the barrel. For a couple of minutes there would be a great commotion of squealing, yelping and flying mash and then silence and I'd lift Silvo out, very pleased with himself, and dispose of the rats.

Ned, who milked the cows, kept greyhounds and fed them rabbits. My 'shooting' was to accompany him when he went out with the gun and carry the rabbits. One day after a long spell of heavy rain the burrows were flooded and the rabbits had to stay on the surface. Ned killed 32 rabbits that day in a short time, but I felt guilty for a long while afterwards because with the flooding the rabbits had no chance of escape. I lay awake that night thinking of them and I never went after rabbits with Ned again. What he did with 32 rabbits I do not know. He probably gave some to neighbours.

I did have one short-lived experience with the gun myself. One day while Captain and Mrs Kemmis were away I went into the gunroom and took down the Captain's rifle and some ammunition. Out in the courtyard I put an old cigarette packet up on a protruding stone on the wall. I went back, took aim and fired. Almost instantaneously I heard the bullet whizzing past my head. I knew what a close thing it had been and in fright I put the gun back immediately and abandoned for ever that particular sport.

The sport I indulged in most was fishing. I made a rod from a bamboo I cut from the grove of bamboos on the riverbank and fished near the house. I would never have asked the Captain to lend me a rod and tackle and flies, so I was most successful when the river was in flood and I fished with the bamboo and the worm. The Captain didn't view fishing with the worm as quite the thing but I didn't learn to fish like a gentleman until much later in life.

Captain and Mrs Kemmis went to church most Sundays and I went with them. On Sundays when they were away or if, for some reason, they weren't going to church I walked down the avenue and turned right onto the road. I called for Matt Boyle, one of the neighbours, and we would make our way past Marty Gleeson's house and cut across the fields on the old Mass path to Holycross. Matt would go on to the chapel beside the ruins of Holycross Abbey and I would take the right fork to Holycross church. The Church of Ireland rector of Thurles and Holycross

was Canon Palmer and the curate was Mr Fox. We sat in the
Armstrong family pew at the front and when three of us were
there we made up approximately a third of the congregation. A
woman played the harmonium and a man with a voice like a
hacksaw behind us sang the hymns on the top of his voice a couple of bars behind the music. Occasionally we went to church in
Thurles where there was a slightly larger congregation of maybe
15 or 20. Going to church gave me a security and a sense of belonging. I never failed to read my Bible and say my prayers. The
Captain had given me a Bible of my own and inscribed it to me. I
read it every night. Reading the Bible wasn't a duty but rather a
fascination. I treasured that Bible; it was the only possession that
was my very own.

One day while I was doing nothing in particular Mrs
Kemmis came and asked me to go for a walk with her. We went
down the laurel walk that led from the far side of the walled garden along a field and down to the river. We were down towards
the end of the paddock when she stopped and said to me:

'What are you going to be when you grow up?' I replied
without hesitation:

'I'm going to be a clergyman.'

'Oh,' she said, 'that could never be.'

From a very young age I always knew I would be ordained. I
had never put it in so many words before. Now that I was put on
the spot I had absolutely no doubt. I had no plans, I didn't know
what I would have to do to achieve it but now that I had articulated it to Mrs Kemmis, despite her negative response, I knew
that somehow that was the course I would take sometime in the
future. Mrs Kemmis never referred to this conversation again
and neither did I, but her reply is etched in my memory.

Sometimes Captain and Mrs Kemmis went to Dublin for the
day and took me with them. We would leave at six o'clock in the
morning and bring sandwiches to eat on the way. They never
used restaurants or hotels. When they went on their own they
left Moyaliffe early and had breakfast in the Kildare Street Club
when they arrived in Dublin. When I was with them they would

drop me within reach of Nelson's Pillar. It was my bearing. If I ever got lost I would make my way back to the Pillar and it was from there I took a bus and would spend the day at Miss Carr's Home where I always received a great welcome. The staff questioned me about how I was getting on; they were interested in the good and the bad. The good – the holidays at Moyaliffe – and the bad – term time at the Havergal. I told them what a horrible man Bifty could be. Until her death in 1970 I used to call from time to time to see Miss Carr. I knew she had a great interest in what I was up to, no matter where I was. I usually called late at night and if she were already in bed one of the staff would go up and tell her, 'Kevin's here.'

'Tell him to come up,' she would say and I would sit beside her bed and we would chat about anything and everything into the small hours of the morning. She knew where most of her children were and especially the girls. She knew how they were getting on and she was concerned for some of them that had problems. Though I never felt a dependence on her I was fond of her and I know she was fond of me.

Captain and Mrs Kemmis went a couple of times during the summer to Ballinacor to keep an eye on things there. During the war, when the car was up on blocks due to the shortage of petrol, they travelled by horse-drawn caravan, staying with friends on the way and taking three days to get from Moyaliffe to Ballinacor. They also did the journey on more than one occasion that I remember by tandem. They had a large tank of petrol buried in a field near the yard, for use in case of emergency, perhaps in case of invasion. I was there after the war when the men dug it up.

After the war they travelled by car to Ballinacor and often took me with them. I slept in a room in the house under the clock tower and helped with jobs around the place. One year on the journey from Moyaliffe the Captain asked me if I would like to take part in a camp. The Reverend Bertie Neill, a Dublin clergyman, brought a group of boys down to a field on Ballinacor for a Scripture Union summer camp. The Captain and Mrs Kemmis encouraged me and I enjoyed the activities of the camp which were mainly walks in the countryside, which of course I knew like the back of my hand, and included an outing to climb Lugnaquilla. There were games and religious activities too.

The religion, which formed an important part of the camp, was mainly hymn singing, Bible study and prayers. Bertie's talks all centred on abandoning sin, getting converted and giving our lives to the Lord. The hymns and prayers and Bible study all referred to the evils of sin, but he was never too specific about what sins he had in mind.

One night after dark I led a troupe of boys from the camp out the back avenue of the house and up to the farmyard where Fitzsimons the steward and his family lived. We climbed over the wall into the garden, went into the glasshouse and helped ourselves to the grapes. We weren't caught red-handed but Bertie and the Kemmises found out. The Captain and Mrs Kemmis forgave me but Bertie was very angry about it. Bertie Neill was a great favourite of Archdeacon Waller who often brought him down to preach in Trinity Church in Limerick. He used to visit the Havergal the following morning and I always enjoyed those visits.

Captain and Mrs Kemmis always went to Ballinacor for the Horse Show in August and often took me with them. During Horse Show Week they had a house party when they and their guests went up to the Show after breakfast and returned in the evening for a late dinner. One day during the Show in 1948 one of the guests was unwell and didn't go to Dublin. Before she left Mrs Kemmis sent for Dr Conniffe who came in due course and left a prescription. The cars were all in Dublin so Corrigan, the butler, sent me on a bike to the chemist in Rathdrum four miles away to have the prescription filled.

I was delighted with the opportunity to go to Rathdrum on my own and I arrived in the village at the top of the hill leading down to the square, full of the joys of spring. It had been two miles uphill from Greenane. After the long push on the stony unmade roads I was glad of the hill down into the village. I picked up speed and sped towards the square. Someone told me afterwards that women standing in their doorways made the sign of the cross as I flew past. When I got into the square I found I couldn't slow down in time to take the corner onto the Main Street. I hit the kerb and crashed headlong into the window of the Post Office. All I remember was lying on the footpath with blood and glass everywhere and a crowd of people around me. I was carted off to the local hospital where I had seventeen stitches in my face and head and the scars are with me ever since. If the houseguest ever got his prescription I never knew.

I was afraid of what Mrs Kemmis might say when she came to see me. As it transpired she was sympathetic, despite the fact that the window cost her £15, and I don't remember but I have no doubt I blamed the brakes of the bike. What I do remember was that while I was in hospital a man and woman I didn't know came to see me. They were the parents of a child that had been on the footpath near the Post Office and was slightly injured by glass when I crashed into the window. They didn't show any great concern for my condition, but as they questioned me about who I was and where I came from I realised they were after money. I wouldn't tell them anything and when they persisted with their questions I thought it was time to cry.

'What are you crying for?' they asked.

'I'm an orphan,' I sobbed, glad for once to be able to turn this to my advantage.

There wasn't another word from them and off they went and I never heard from them again.

I was in hospital for ten days and returned to Ballinacor in the middle of the harvest, and I revelled in the great sympathy I received from everybody. Mrs Kemmis had contacted the Havergal to say I would be late back. While I recovered from the accident I had no responsibilities and I enjoyed the peace and tranquillity of Ballinacor. I wandered out the back gate and up the hill through the bracken. From the top I looked down to the house and grounds and across the valley to the random patchwork of fields of cut and uncut corn and of green pastures dotted with cattle. Behind and below was the lake bordered with frock-ens. Trees in the hedgerows – Scots pine, sycamore, ash and oak – added to the scene that was a long way from the Havergal.

As I did in Moyaliffe I came to know the neighbours in some of the nearby cottages. In one of these the family told me the Kemmises had the goodwill of the local people because they had bought Ballinacor and had not taken it.

Sometimes I took the bicycle and cycled as far as Glenmalure. It was quite a push but the satisfaction of getting there made the hard work worthwhile. If I had money for lemonade or an ice cream I would sit by the river and then cycle home.

That year, after about three weeks extension to my holiday for convalescence, without returning to Moyaliffe, one of the men drove me to the train for Dublin and from there I took the train to Limerick to endure another term of Bifty and the Havergal.

I enjoyed Ballinacor but I loved Moyaliffe and, despite the difference between the Kemmises and me, I was attached to them. They were, I believe, fond of me too and they were good to me according to their own lights. The people who worked on Moyaliffe were also important to me. They were mostly people without pretension, country people contented to do an honest day's work for what must have been a meagre wage. Some of them worked parttime on Moyaliffe and they looked forward to the beet campaign when there was extra work at the factory in Thurles with much better pay, but of course the work was seasonal.

Most of them lived close to the estate and I was welcome in their homes when I called, as I often did. In one house, O'Keeffe's, if they weren't at home, I used to let myself in through the window and listen to records on the wind-up gramophone. If there were potatoes in the pot by the fire, I'd help myself, add a big knob of butter and have a feed, and this was accepted as normal by the woman of the house. If I called to a cottage at mealtime a place was set for me at the table without comment and I was in-

cluded as if I were one of the family. I sat to their firesides at
night and listened to the talk of the day and met neighbours who
came rambling and talked about their great passion, hurling. I
was often terrified on the way back to Moyaliffe on a dark night
after a session of ghost stories at somebody's fireside. Sometimes my route was the one I took with the postbag earlier in the
day – I crossed the coffin-stile, whistled past the graveyard, ran
through the field, crossed the lawn and tip-toed over the gravel
to the yard and the safety of my bed.

Before I went back to the Havergal after the long summer
holidays at Moyaliffe I used to go around to say goodbye to all
the workmen and many of them gave me a shilling as I left. A
shilling out of a farm labourer's wage of the time was a generous
gift to a young boy who wasn't even a relation. One year I remember arriving back at the school with my short trousers
weighed down with shillings, afraid they'd fall through my
pocket. With one of these shillings I bought a brand new foun-
tain-pen from one of the other boys. Soon after that another boy
arrived back after the holidays and I sold it to him for two
shillings. I might have done well in business!

John O'Connor, the butler, was particularly kind. He slept in
the room next to me in the servants' quarters. One night there
was a big thunderstorm and I lay awake frightened out of my
wits. I heard John's voice:

'Are you all right there?'

'Yes,' I said trying to be brave.

He knew I was frightened and in a few minutes he said to me:

'You can come into my bed if you want to.'

I went in and got in beside him and stayed for an hour or
more until the storm had passed. He said or did nothing unto-
ward, only gave me comfort when I was frightened.

At the end of the holidays either Marty Gleeson drove me to
the bus in Rosmult in the horse and cart or John O'Connor took
me on the bar of his bike to the train in Goold's Cross. When I
went with John we'd stop at a pub in Goold's Cross where he'd
have a bottle of stout and buy me a bottle of lemonade.

I don't remember telling the other boys of my times at Moyaliffe and Ballinacor in any great detail but I have no doubt they asked me questions and I told them. I also have no doubt that anything I did tell them must have seemed exotic, for any of them who did have holidays away from the Havergal did not have anywhere like Moyaliffe to go to.

I was not aware of it at the time, and I certainly did not set out to do so, but my stories of Moyaliffe and Ballinacor must have given rise to envy or jealousy among some of the other boys. I do remember my Bible, the gift from the Captain, being my proud possession and I may have said so. One day in the school one of the older boys by the name of Albert McKeon, from Armagh, called me to follow him out into the yard. He was grinning and beckoning to me. I was sure he was going to show me some great secret. I followed him around the side of the house where he lifted the lid to the main sewer and indicated to me to look in. He stood grinning at me as I looked down and there lying in the sewage was my Bible. I was devastated.

How people can set out to be cruel to each other I could never understand. It is said that when children are cruel to each other, as they often are, it is part of growing up, part of learning about people and the world. This may be, but there is no excuse for adults to set out to be cruel to each other and certainly no excuse for adults to be cruel to children, and of course mental cruelty is far worse than physical cruelty. One day in religion class Bifty was reading something and came across the word 'bastard'.

'Do any of you know what that word means?' he asked. Nobody answered.

'Answer, you amadáns,' he said, 'some of you must know.' Still no answer.

'Dalton, you tell me, you should know what the word 'bastard' means.' I sang dumb. I knew what it meant, but I wasn't going to give him the satisfaction, and going around in my head was that it was he that was the real bastard. He asked me again, so in the end I said to him:

'Naw, I don't know.' He hated when we said 'naw' for 'no'.

He used to say it was ignorant and we knew it would get him going and he would lose his temper.

'Boy,' he said, 'never answer me like that again or I'll teach you a lesson you won't forget. You'll never be any good for anything,' he went on, 'you can't even speak properly. Look at him with a vacant expression on his face like a bullock looking over a five-barred gate,' but he didn't get me to say it.

CHAPTER FIVE

Hens and Eggs

In early 1949, when I was sixteen, one day out of the blue Bifty sent for me. My usual reaction when he wanted me was not, 'What have I done now?' but 'What has he found out now?' I prepared myself for yet another confrontation, although, be it said, he hit me less often as I got older.

'I've had a letter from Miss Carr. Those people in Tipperary are starting a poultry farm and you're going to work for them.' I wasn't consulted, I had no say in the matter but I'd have gone almost anywhere to get away from the Havergal, and I'm sure that by this time Bifty was glad to get rid of me. This was presented to me as a *fait accompli* but I was delighted as Moyaliffe was the only other life I knew and I loved being there. Mrs Kemmis had been in touch with the Archdeacon and Miss Carr and this is what they had decided.

At the time, James Dillon was Minister for Agriculture in the inter-party government. A great parliamentarian and an orator of the old school, he devised a scheme for Ireland, as he said, 'to drown Britain in eggs'. He gave substantial subsidies to people to establish poultry farms in pursuit of this colourful ambition. The Kemmises took the bait and planned to set up a unit at Moyaliffe. They had the space and with minimum labour cost, paying me less than they would pay a man, they saw they could make money. They wanted me to run the project in return for my keep, two and sixpence a week and two and a half per cent of the profits. I jumped at the opportunity to leave the Havergal, and especially to get to Moyaliffe fulltime. For this I would nearly have worked for nothing, but not quite!

When I was leaving the Archdeacon decided that before I

went I must be confirmed. Two years before I had told him I did
not want to be confirmed, something that was unheard of in
those days – that a child should question the system and make a
decision for himself on such a matter. My refusal caused quite a
stir but in the end I won out. I'm not sure exactly why I did not
want to be confirmed; I simply didn't feel ready, but when it
came to the following year and leaving the Havergal for good, I
agreed. I think I would have agreed to anything to get away
from there and away from Bifty.

The Archdeacon arranged with the bishop of the diocese,
Bishop Hodges, to confirm me at a hastily arranged service in
Trinity Church the night before I was to leave. These two ecclesi-
astics didn't get on well together as I believe the Archdeacon,
after almost fifty years in Limerick, thought he should have been
bishop. At the service there were the three of us, two or three
other people from the parish I didn't know, and the organist.

Bishop Hodges was a small spare sparrow-like man and I remember vividly kneeling in front of him while he confirmed me.
He was a good preacher and for my confirmation he based his
sermon on the hymn:

> Jesus bids us shine with a pure, clear light,
> Like a little candle burning in the night:
> In this world of darkness so we must shine,
> You in your small corner, and I in mine.

His point was that wherever life took the Christian or whatever
he ended up doing, he should be a light shining in the dark
places of the world. I haven't always shone very brightly but I
have never forgotten that sermon.

I had no sentiment about leaving the Havergal. I have no
memory of the day I left or of saying goodbye to Bifty or to anybody else. After seven years, despite the tough regime that it
was, it might be thought that I would have some small hint of
sadness, but no, I was delighted to be leaving it. What I do remember is being totally focused on what lay ahead, the expectation, the excitement.

I knew nothing about hens and eggs other than collecting

eggs from the hens kept for the house in Moyaliffe. A child who hasn't collected eggs in a henhouse has missed something in life. This however wasn't enough to put me in charge of a commercial poultry farm, so Mrs Kemmis arranged for me to go straight from Limerick to Dublin to learn about hens, chickens and eggs. Miss Carr had a hand in organising it and arranged for me to stay in Ranelagh with a family called Laycock, which I thought was amusing considering what I was there to learn. The Laycocks were kind to me and every day I went to Livestock Foods in North King Street, where the boss was a Dr Senior and I learned, as I thought, all there was to be known on the subject. I learned how to mix growers mash, layers mash and every other kind of mash and how much to feed to hens of various sizes, ages and conditions. One day we were about to mix tons of a particular kind of mash when the foreman sent me to the office in a hurry to ask for two eggs and a glass hammer to break them into the mix. I went down to the office like a fool and came back and told him innocently that the girl only laughed at me.

At the end of the two weeks I took the train to Thurles where the Captain met me and brought me to Moyaliffe to run the new project, and in no time I was up to my eyes in Rhode Island Red and Light Sussex hens. I was back permanently in the place in the world I loved most of all and felt secure, where I knew everybody and was on good terms with them all. I was back in my own room in the servants' quarters and it took me a while to get used to the idea that never again would I be getting on the bus or train to return to the Havergal and to the terrible Bifty and his unjust and brutal ways.

The work of the poultry farm consisted of buying-in day-old chicks and rearing them up in hoovers. These were square containers with an oil lamp in the middle to provide the necessary heat for the chicks to thrive. When they got to a certain stage we moved them out to the folds in the field, and later when the cockerels came to a certain weight we sold them off and the pullets we kept for laying. My job was to ensure a steady temperature for the chicks and to feed them and the hens and clean them out and move the folds every day so that the hens had fresh grass to pick.

I could not have been happier looking after the hens and producing the eggs. If Captain and Mrs Kemmis were away I had a lie-in and the hens had to wait until 10.30 or 11.00 am to be looked after. I drove a donkey and cart. Brownie was the donkey and on the cart there was a forty-gallon drum to bring water out to the hens, and I whistled and sang the whole day long and employed Silvo to kill the rats. If I finished my jobs before the end of the working day I used to go into the garden to talk to the gardeners or help one of the other men around the yard with whatever they were doing. One day when the Kemmises were away a lady, a friend of theirs, arrived. She was a very proper member of 'the quality' and she wanted to buy as she said 'A gentleman hen'. I laughed inside myself at the thought of her not wanting to use the word 'cock'. Anyhow I gave her her 'gentleman hen', and off she went happy with her well-bred self.

In the spring when the clocks were put forward an hour to give an extra hour's daylight, many country people didn't observe this 'new time'. They kept to what they called 'old time', and this was the custom at Moyaliffe. On one or two occasions there was 'double summer time'. Some of the older people referred to 'old time', 'new time' and 'God's time'. It was all very confusing. Country people felt that the State had no right to interfere in such matters and doing so would bring its own judgment, like bad weather.

Jimmy Dwyer and Jimmy Fitzgerald were two of the men that always had their lunch in the kitchen. Jimmy Dwyer, before he entered the kitchen, always put his head around the door and said:

'God bless all here.' The reply came:

'You too.' Then he'd ask:

'Any news?' and he'd come in and sit down at the table. His routine was the same every day. I learned much from the conversation at these meals. It ranged over matters of the estate, local gossip, hurling, the state of the country and the world at large. The great source of information was the wireless news that provided the material for learned comments from the men. However, the favourite programme was Hospitals Requests, and if John McCormack came on singing 'Bless This House' Jimmy Fitzgerald would become all solemn and demand total silence from everyone. Jimmy Dwyer eventually went to America and I attended his American wake, a tradition that went back to famine times when a person going away was waked as if dead, as there was no expectation of seeing them again.

Kate Healy, the cook, produced and served the meals. Kate was in her sixties. She was small, thin and frail. She wore a shapeless black dress and a white band across the front of her head, like a bandage, tied at the nape of her neck. She moved slowly around the kitchen and when she spoke she had a thin quiet voice. When she was younger her whole family had emigrated to America but Kate failed the medical and was left behind. She played a violin at night when she scratched out the same tunes, 'Turkey in the Straw', 'The Rakes of Mallow,' and a few more. Every Sunday morning and holy day of obligation, before breakfast, hail rain or snow, Kate walked the three miles to 8 o'clock Mass in Drumbane. Once a year, in the summer, she went for her two weeks holiday to Co Limerick, where exactly, and to whom, nobody knew.

Kate's presence in the kitchen kept the men's conversation within reasonable bounds, though she was capable, in her quiet way, of holding her own. One day John O'Connor had a photograph of a beauty competition from a Sunday newspaper, of young women in bathing costumes. The men were ogling the photograph when Kate put a bowl of potatoes in the middle of the table and said quietly, to nobody in particular, as she walked back to the range, 'Pity they have to shit.'

As when I had been at Moyaliffe on holiday, at night time I used to ramble to the houses of the families I knew and that knew me well. Like the conversations in the kitchen, I listened rather than talked and learned a lot about the ways of people and of the world.

Around this time I came to know Des Hanafin and his family. His father, an Old IRA man, originally from Longford, was a small trader in Thurles and a Fianna Fáil County Councillor. As a Councillor he worked hard for the people of the town. The Town Commissioners put street lighting outside the Roman Catholic Cathedral in Thurles, and some Church of Ireland parishioners asked that the roadway to their church be similarly lit. There were local objections to this, but Des's father fought hard to have it done and succeeded – a manifestation of his true republicanism. Tipperary North Riding County Council granted three university scholarships annually to be taken up at one of the colleges of the National University. During Des's own time as chairman of the Council a proposal was made that should a Protestant win a scholarship he or she would be free to take it up at a university of their choice. The proposal was defeated by 18 votes to 3. Des was one of the three who voted for the motion. Like father like son.

Mr Hanafin had a paper shop called 'The Corner Shop'. I found my way there to buy *The Dandy*, *The Beano* and *The Wizard*, and it was there I met Des when he was home on holiday from Rockwell College, and we became friends. We spent a lot of time arguing about religion but I never made inroads into his conviction that the Roman Catholic Church was the one true church. Through Des I got to know Binky, his sister, and his mother and father and spent many evenings in Hanafin's house where I always felt welcome. They were one of the few people I told about Bifty and the Havergal.

I used to cycle the nine miles to Thurles at night to go to the pictures, and then call in to Hanafins to have an argument with Des about religion. When I left, he would walk the half mile or so with me as far as the hospital for company and we would continue the argument. Years later Binky told me she remembered him arriving home red in the face and saying about some point or other, 'I'm going to go after him for that, I'm not going to let him away with it.'

I had been working on the poultry farm about nine months

when I got a pain in the heel of my left foot. It persisted and I found it difficult to walk. Captain and Mrs Kemmis brought me to Dublin to Sir Patrick Dun's Hospital to see Mr Gill, the surgeon. He had my foot X-rayed and diagnosed a bad bruise. He said it would be all right in a few weeks. Instead of improving it got worse until it became evident there was an infection. We went back to Mr Gill who diagnosed osteomyelitis and arranged to operate the following morning. Antibiotics had recently become available and I was on a heavy dose of them in hospital for three weeks, and when I returned to Moyaliffe my leg was in plaster for a further six weeks. I was one of the lucky ones and made a full recovery. Two other Havergal boys I knew had the same infection and one of them had a short leg for the rest of his life. I believe that malnutrition is a factor in the development of this disease.

It was only around this time I began to reflect on my relationship with the Kemmises and how I thought they understood their relationship with me. My situation now was different from when I went to Moyaliffe first. It was clear that my status in their eyes changed after the morning of the incident when the Captain was almost overcome on the way back to his dressing-room. Before this I was included in the events of the house, I ate in the dining room with Captain and Mrs Kemmis, Mrs Kemmis bathed me at night and made sure I said my prayers, I slept in a bedroom beside the Captain's dressing-room and I was generally part of the family. After that event I slept and ate in the servants' quarters and spent my time there. This was all quite normal to me at the time. I was young and so different was everything to me I was happy to accept whatever happened. It was only in retrospect that I became aware of the change and speculated on its significance and its cause.

Years later the widow of one of the stewards, who still lived on the place, told me that Captain and Mrs Kemmis considered the possibility of adopting me but Mrs Kemmis's mother who lived in England was against it, presumably on the grounds that if Mrs Kemmis and the Captain had nobody to leave Moyaliffe to, then one of her grandchildren would be in line to inherit. I have no way of knowing whether any of this was other than pure speculation and they never led me to believe that this might be the case. There was no way of anybody knowing what was in the minds of the Kemmises, and I'm certain that they would not have talked to or given the slightest hint, even unintentionally, to any of the staff. From the sequence of events they may have considered the possibility of adopting an heir for Moyaliffe but decided I didn't measure up or such a thing may never have been in their minds. Either way they were good to me and provided a security for me at a critical stage of my life that I would never forget.

In Moyaliffe at this time I was something of an anomaly to the rest of the staff. I was neither one thing nor the other. I had lived in the house with Captain and Mrs Kemmis in the past. I had spent time with them when I was there on holiday in previous years. I used to go to Dublin with them and to stay at Ballinacor. Now that I was employed I was answerable directly to Mrs Kemmis and didn't come under the steward. Everybody, including myself, was happy with this arrangement and it had advantages for me. I was freer and happier sleeping and eating in the servants' quarters than I would have been in the house, and since I wasn't under the steward, when Captain and Mrs Kemmis weren't around I was able to, more or less, make my own time, provided I got through the work. When they were away and I took the odd lie-in in the morning and might not have worked to the bell in the evening there was nobody to say anything to me. The staff, who didn't seem to mind what I did, accepted my anomalous situation.

By the time I was eighteen and had been running the poultry farm for about two years, I began to think about the future. I still dreamed about being ordained, the dream that kept coming up since I was a boy. I had no idea what this would involve but the thought of being ordained kept recurring. I was comfortable and happy at Moyaliffe but I was aware there was a great big world out there and sooner or later I would have to enter it if I were to make this dream of mine come true. At Moyaliffe I was particularly friendly with the children of Mr O'Neill, the steward. Iris, one of his daughters, had gone to London to train as a nurse at Charing Cross Hospital and wrote to me regularly telling me all about her life there. This gave me a picture of the outside world and I in turn used to write back and keep her up to date with the gossip and the goings-on around Moyaliffe.

I was beginning to feel unsettled when another critical incident in my life occurred that helped me to decide that the time had come for me to leave Moyaliffe. I was in the bathroom of the servants' quarters one day when I heard the Captain outside saying to Mrs Kemmis, 'That boy is absolutely useless.' I was devastated. It had come from the Captain for whom I had a great respect and affection.

It was the only snatch of conversation I heard and I have no idea what I had done or not done that the Captain thought I was useless. It confirmed me in my view that it was time to go and so I wrote to Miss Carr and told her I wanted to leave. Miss Carr was in periodic touch with Mrs Kemmis and since my original contact with her and the Captain had been through Miss Carr, I thought this was the best thing to do.

Miss Carr wrote to the Kemmises to tell them and the morning the letter arrived the Captain came to me in the yard. He told me he was sorry I wanted to leave and he would do everything he could to help me. He thought he might be able to get me a job in Guinness's as he knew the managing director well. Later that day Mrs Kemmis arrived. She was angry and asked me did I know how ungrateful I was. She told me she knew all about the time I turned over the horse and cart, and did I realise that when I rode into the Post Office in Rathdrum on the bicycle it cost her £15 to replace the window, and then she turned on her heel and went off in as high dudgeon as her five feet nothing allowed. Her attitude distressed me greatly but did not deflect me from my determination to leave.

After a while I had heard nothing further. I have no doubt that Mrs Kemmis decided that if they let the matter sit I would change my mind. The opposite was in fact the case. As time passed I was confirmed in my view that to leave Moyaliffe and take my chances in Dublin was the right thing to do. So one day I managed to go to Dublin and see Miss Carr and tell her I really did want to leave Moyaliffe. Soon after this, arrangements were made for me to go to Dublin. A few days before I was due to leave the Captain came to wish me well and gave me my insurance card stamped to date and a five-pound note, a generous gift to a boy in those days.

When the day arrived Mrs Kemmis and the Captain were away so they arranged with Johnny McGlynn to take me in the horse and cart to the train, but something arose and I had to wait another week. On the actual day I left Moyaliffe the leading text in my *Daily Light* book of Bible readings for that morning was: 'Lo I am with you always.' This gave me great confidence. It was powerfully meaningful to me, especially on that particular day and I never forgot it. This was the autumn of 1951.

CHAPTER SIX

The Harding

The Harding Technical Institute in Lord Edward Street was a working boys' hostel, affectionately known to its residents as 'The Ranch', run by a man called Nobby Clarke. It was founded in 1878 to provide accommodation and training in the technical trades for boys, mostly Protestant, between the ages of 16 and 21 years. By the 1950s the training side of the Harding had ceased and it was simply a hostel that provided accommodation for Protestant boys of limited means, mostly from the country, who worked in Dublin.

It was a substantial red brick building with a long frontage at the top of Lord Edward Street. Inside there was a large hall with the kitchen at the far end with a hatch to the dining-room on the left. To the right there was a passage that led to another passage to the back yard, off which there was a washroom with showers and handbasins. In the yard there was an entrance from outside from where our bicycles were stolen. There was quite a grand staircase to the first floor. To the left at the top of the stairs were the billiard room, study room and the secretary's office. On the right there was a hall for badminton that was used from time to time for plays and concerts. Further on were Nobby's sitting-room and bedroom. On the second floor there were dormitories with ten or twelve young men in each dormitory, and another dormitory above these.

The facilities were basic but adequate – a good bed with breakfast, and dinner in the evening. The snooker table provided amusement for residents who had little money to spend on entertainment in the city. Boys paid for their keep according to their income.

When I arrived in Dublin Miss Carr brought me straight to the Harding to meet Nobby. He was a former British Army captain who held himself straight. He was a slightly built man of medium height with a pleasant face. He was kind, and good with the young men. He was ideal for the job but expected a moderate amount of discipline. He was not above threatening to put a boy out if he was not behaving, and with one of the residents while I was there, he carried out the threat.

All I had was the five pounds the Captain had given me before I left Moyaliffe and a few shillings I had saved. Nobby was reassuring and told me, 'I'll keep you here until you get a job. Don't worry.'

I warmed to the man immediately and felt confident that if I didn't get a job myself he would be able to get one for me. This was 1951 when there were few jobs to be had. Unemployment was endemic and thousands of people were emigrating to find work. I wasn't conscious of the overall picture and without having much idea of what I was doing, I pounded the footpaths of Dublin calling to shops and businesses looking for work. I realised I would have to take whatever I could get for I was conscious of having only a primary education and never having passed an exam. I hid my torn trousers and my scruffy clothes with a long overcoat. After two months of no success I was demoralised to the point that I considered going to England, for I still had the £5 the Captain gave me to pay the fare.

Then one morning Nobby came down to me in the snooker room. 'Kevin, there's a man on the phone who says he knows you.' Williams was a man of about sixty who had adopted a boy from Miss Carr's Home called Tommy. He had a glass, paint and hardware business in Cathedral Street, in the heart of Dublin opposite the side of the Pro-Cathedral, a few yards from Nelson's Pillar.

'He has a job going and he wants you to go down and see him,' said Nobby. My heart lifted. I knew something would turn up. Then Nobby said, 'I don't think you should go. He won't pay you properly. He's no good.'

On the principle that something is better than nothing I decided to go. Williams talked to me about Miss Carr's and recounted how he remembered me. He offered me a job for thirty shillings a week, working in the shop, the store and, when needed, on the lorry. Despite what Nobby had said I decided to take it. It was a start.

I learned about different kinds of glass and how to cut it to size. Sometimes I helped Mr Benn and Mr Brown behind the counter in the shop or I was sent up to a store Williams had in a lane off Parnell Square to help there. The thing I remember most about the three months I worked there was the amount of time I spent on the back of the open pick-up truck making deliveries around the city. Williams got an order for glass for new houses under construction in Sallynoggin, and three or four times a week for a couple of months we made the journey to the building site. My job was to stand on the back of the truck to steady the containers that held the glass so they didn't shift with the movement of the truck in the traffic, not that in those days there was much traffic in Dublin. I hated it but it was one of the best things that ever happened me. Any false sense I may have had of my own importance disappeared as I stood performing this menial task on the back of the truck, on display for the whole world to see.

I came to know the hardware trade fairly well in the time I was there, but I knew I wouldn't stay even in the short term. There was no future in it. It was a dead end. Williams didn't pay me enough to live on. There were holes in the soles of my shoes and the backside was out of my trousers. Of the £1.10s I earned I paid £1 to Nobby for my keep and had ten shillings for myself. On the first week I was paid I left the ten shillings in my coat pocket and somebody stole it. Ten shillings wasn't enough for me to get by on anyway, so after a few weeks I went in to see Williams.

'I want a rise.'

'What's that?' he said.

'I want more money.'

'Oh, I couldn't afford that. What do you want more money for?'

'I want to buy a pair of shoes. Look at that.' I said, holding up my foot and showing him a big hole in the sole.

'I'll give you a chit and you can go up to Tylers and they'll give you a pair of shoes.'

So I went up to Tylers in O'Connell Street and had half the stock of the shop on the floor. Eventually I settled on a pair. A few weeks later Williams came to me.

'Look at this,' he said, waving an invoice above his head.

'Come into my office.' I followed him into his office where he pushed the offending piece of paper at me.

'Never do that again.'

'Never do what again?'

'If I ever send you to Tylers for shoes again get ordinary shoes not the best shoes in the shop.'

In those days there was nothing about a five-day week. I worked on Saturday mornings in the shop and as a condition of employment I had to work in Williams's garden at his home at the top of Collins Avenue on Saturday afternoons with no extra pay. He was a religious man who gave a lot of his money to missions and evangelical organisations rather than pay his staff a reasonable wage. It was also said that he used to try to convert Roman Catholics who worked for him, showing great concern for the state of their immortal souls. He made it a condition of giving me the job that I join Christian Endeavour, the same evangelical organisation for saving souls that ran the holiday home in Kilkee. I went a few times and decided it wasn't my cup of tea and never went back again, but Williams never said anything to me about it. He demanded, however, that I write essays for him on biblical topics. When he read one of these essays on St John's gospel he asked:

'Are you sure you wrote this yourself?'

'Of course I did,' I said, and he went off muttering to himself: 'Amazing, amazing.'

The people who worked for Williams were mostly

Protestants. They were a decent bunch of people to work with, except for Jim Kaplan the driver of the lorry, especially when he came into work the worse for the previous night's drink. When he had a hangover you could see it on his face. He used bad language at the best of times, but when he had a hangover it was foul. I don't believe I ever heard anyone to match him.

I decided I wasn't going to go on working for Williams and spent what time I could applying for other jobs. I went for a couple of interviews on two successive Saturdays but without success. At one of these interviews in a small Dublin factory I thought I had done well and I was sure I would get the job. I was undermined completely a week later when a letter arrived to say that I hadn't. A few days after that Nobby Clarke came to me to tell me that the man who had interviewed me, Jim Ellis, whose father had been in the same regiment in the war as Nobby, had been on the phone to ask him to tell me not to be too disappointed as nobody had been appointed. I was glad of this kindness and it lifted my spirits and my optimism returned. A couple of days later Jim Ellis rang Nobby again to tell me he had arranged an interview for me in the Dublin Port Milling Company in Alexandra Road. It transpired that the small Dublin factory that Jim Ellis ran was near the Mill and was a subsidiary of it.

Jim Ellis had arranged the interview for 11.30 am on the following Saturday. That morning I was working with Jim Kaplan, the driver, who was badly hung over from the night before.

'Get that glass up on the back of the lorry,' he shouted.

'I can't Jim, I'm not going with you today.'

'You are f…ing coming with me to-day.'

'No,' I said, 'I'm not. I'm going for an interview.'

'Well I'm going to ring the f…ing boss.'

'Ring him away.' I said, and he did.

'What do you mean he's going for an interview?' Williams asked him on the phone. 'Put him on to me,' and Kaplan handed me the phone.

'What's this I hear about you and an interview?'

'I have an interview at half past eleven and I can't go on the lorry.'

'What do you mean you have an interview?'

'I'm looking for another job.'

'Stay there till I come up,' he said, and in ten minutes he arrived up at the store off Parnell Square. He was his usual blustering self.

'What's all this about?'

'I'm going for an interview,' I said, 'I'm looking for another job.'

'Does Miss Carr know about this?'

'No,' I said.

'Does Mr Clarke?'

'Yes.'

'And what does he say?'

'He says I'm right.'

'If you go for this interview you needn't come back here, there'll be no job for you.'

'That's all right,' I said. He persisted.

'Do you understand? If you don't get this job you needn't come back here. You'll be out of work. Unemployed.'

'That's OK,' I said and cycled off down the lane with the backside of my trousers waving in the breeze and Williams shouting after me:

'You don't know when you're well off.'

I went back to the Harding, cleaned myself up and cycled down to the Port Mill.

My appointment was with a Mr Milliken, the Company Secretary. He was a Northern Presbyterian and a polite and friendly man. He brought me into his office and asked me to sit down. One of Jim Ellis's staff from Procea was working in the wheat intake of the mill and Ellis wanted him back so he gave Milliken my name as a possible replacement. As soon as I reasonably could I let Milliken know that in coming for the interview I had lost my job with Williams. He asked me a lot of questions about myself and where I came from. I told him as much as I wanted to, but some of my story I invented. I told him my parents had been killed in Liverpool in the bombing during the war.

This is what I used to say if I was put on the spot. He then told me about the job and conditions and about subsidised meal tickets for the canteen. Then out of the blue he simply said:

'We'll give you three months trial and pay you £3.10s a week and start on Monday.'

It wasn't a case of 'We'll write and let you know'. He came straight out with it: 'We'll give you three months trial …' I assumed Jim Ellis had talked to him about me. I couldn't believe it. It was to prove the biggest break I ever had. In a sense I never looked back after I got that job. As I cycled back to the Harding I calculated that I would probably have the best part of £2 a week to myself after my keep, and laughed at the thought of Williams doing his own garden that afternoon.

I started work in the Port Mill on 3 March 1952. I was put to work on the intake where wheat coming in was recorded. My boss was Mick O'Connor who had joined up for the First World War at the age of sixteen and came through the five years, including the trenches, without a scratch. I had fallen on my feet. Over the first weekend I was there I got a crippling dose of flu. I couldn't go to work for a whole week and I was sure I'd be fired, but I didn't hear anything. I went to work the following week unsure of myself and not only was I not fired, but I was paid for the week I was sick. By that one deed they had secured my loyalty.

Working in the Port Mill was undoubtedly one of the best breaks I ever had. It was a large firm employing almost 200 people. At first I worked as a checker in the intake department. The men wheeled sacks of wheat in from a wagon that ran on tracks outside and put them on a weighing scale. I had to record the weight of each sack, take random samples and then the men emptied the sacks into a hopper. The wheat was then dried and stored in bins in the silo from where it was blended with imported wheat to make bakers or home-baking flour.

A couple of years later Mick O'Connor died and I was put in charge of the intake for the coming season. I was delighted with myself. Shortly after the season started the boss, P. D. Odlum, appeared one day at the intake. He was a tall good-looking man and he wore a white coat. He strolled around and I knew by him he wasn't missing much. He came into the office and we discussed the quality of the new season's wheat and its suitability for making flour. I found him pleasant and easy to talk to but I was well aware that he was the boss and chairman of the company.

Authority figures have never greatly impressed me, having dealt with such diverse chiefs as Mrs Kemmis, Bifty and the Archdeacon. I learned from dealing with them that if you didn't stand up for yourself nobody else would. Despite the fact that he was the boss, I liked P. D. Odlum from the start, and that made it easy for me to talk to him as naturally as I would to one of the checkers. When I opened my pay packet the following Friday there was an extra £2 in it; he had seen that my new job had brought me new responsibility and had acknowledged it. With the next annual rise a couple of months later I was earning £9. 10s a week, which was a good wage for an unqualified worker of twenty-two years of age in 1954. Things were looking up.

I did not have a plan as to how or when I would begin to enquire about being ordained. My increased income in a job I found fascinating tended to push the idea to the back of my mind. Furthermore, the hurdle of passing the matriculation exam to enter Trinity at times made the dream seem almost impossible. For long periods I never thought about it at all, but it was there in the background. I still said my prayers and read my Bible and went to church every Sunday and all these things were important to me, but I enjoyed my work at the mill and my ultimate ambition took a back seat.

Some of the boys in the Harding worked in banks or insurance companies. Some worked in Protestant firms like Parkes of the Coombe, Dockrells and Brooks Thomas. These Protestant firms were a start for boys who hadn't got leaving certificates but they paid badly. I was told that they were good at awarding titles of responsibility without awarding corresponding increases in pay. I was fortunate to get a job with the Port Mill that prided itself on paying their employees on a par with the banks.

My first Christmas in the Harding was bleak, though I don't

remember much about it. I had nowhere to go, and as I had made the break with Moyaliffe I wouldn't have considered going back. On Christmas Eve Golding Kidd, one of the other residents, wished me a happy Christmas on his way out to get the bus home for the holidays. Twenty minutes later he arrived back to tell me he was sorry he couldn't bring me with him. For a number of years after that I went home with Golding to Moyne, Co Wicklow every Christmas and Easter. There was a big family all home for the holiday and there was great fun and a lot of banter. The Kidds were kind people. Golding's mother was very Protestant and read the *Protestant Telegraph* and approved of much of what Mr Paisley said and quoted him frequently. I used to argue with her, but didn't always win. Despite her extreme religious views she was a good woman with a warm heart who treated me as one of the family.

Life was not all hard work. The Harding had a cricket club that played at Londonbridge Road. Most of the others learned their cricket at secondary school; many of them were keen and some of them were good at the game. As the Havergal and cricket were in different worlds I was never more than 12th man on the Harding second team, and no matter who dropped out I never moved any nearer to getting a game. My contribution was to make the tea, for which service George Mooney used to assure me that I would be mentioned in despatches at the AGM. I could never play any sport, possibly because I hadn't played as a child, or possibly because I was no good at sports anyway. I did however have one notable sporting achievement.

There was a Harding sports day at Londonbridge Road every summer at which Johnny Doonan was a specialist in the mile race. Doonan was a conservative evangelical Christian who seemed to specialise in what evangelicals call backsliding. This meant that from time to time he would go off the straight and narrow, take drink, dance, go to the pictures and play cards. Then the error of his ways would get the better of him, he would be full of remorse and commit himself again to the Lord and exhort the rest of us to do the same. When he was in this state he was intolerable. He knew my broad church leanings and I became one of his prime targets. I couldn't bear it. His theological position was inimical to my middle of the road Anglicanism, and I found it hard to like the fellow, especially when he was in the saved state, although to be fair to him when he was backsliding he was good company. I was determined to take him on in his own speciality, the mile race, at the next Harding sports.

At this stage I knocked around with a fellow called Cyril Roleston who was always tormenting me to take a cigarette. Eventually one day, to shut him up, I took one and cursed the day for twenty-five years until I finally kicked the habit. The first thing I did in training for the race was to give up the cigarettes. I took a raw egg every second morning and went out training on the roads at six o'clock every morning, often with some of the lads pacing me on a bicycle. In order to account for my early mornings the rumour circulated in the Ranch that I was involved with the IRA and Johnny Doonan swallowed it.

I intended to beat Doonan and I took the whole thing seriously. I cannot remember now exactly why it meant so much to me to win. It may have been because I believed that if I beat him in the mile I would establish the superiority of my kind of religion over his, or it may have been that in all of the sport going on around me I simply wanted to win at something. After a good deal of lost sweat, early nights and early mornings the day arrived. There were at least a dozen others in the race, but as far as I was concerned there were only two: Doonan and Dalton. I didn't know much about tactics, in fact I knew nothing about them, but relied on my own native cunning. In the early stages I kept Doonan within easy reach. I wasn't going to show my hand too soon so I stayed behind for a few laps and then pulled up the field. On the last lap I went ahead and took the lead, but I knew I was tiring. I felt it not in my wind but in my legs.

I stayed in front and as I came around the last bend my legs were giving out. I heard Dudgeon on the sideline shouting, 'Dalton's going to win it.' Then I heard the pounding of feet coming closer behind me and my legs were nearly gone, but I said to myself, 'This bugger's not going to beat me,' and found from somewhere the energy to keep ahead and win. To my amazement it was Kidd that was behind me and came second and Doonan was third. The no cigarettes, the early mornings, the raw eggs and I suppose the determination had paid off.

After the race Joe Blain, who was a serious athlete, a member of Donore Harriers, came over and asked me if I would join Donore. 'You know you did that mile in under five minutes' he told me, and that was before the four-minute mile had been broken. I wasn't interested but I was delighted with the congratulations of the others and in an evil kind of way I was most pleased of all that I had beaten Doonan.

At night after dinner in the Harding, if there was nothing else to do Fred Buttimore and I used to go down to Cafolla's Café in O'Connell Street for one of those huge knickerbocker glory ice-creams and a cup of coffee, and listen to Marilyn Monroe on the juke-box singing 'I'm Just a Little Girl from Littlerock'. It was a carefree time but we considered a trip to Cafolla's self-indulgent.

Golding Kidd used to go to dances in The Protestant Hall on Northumberland Road. I went with him a couple of times because Mary, a girl I was keen on, used to go there too. On one of the nights I went she wasn't there and I left another girl home to a flat in Waterloo Road. It was a cold night and she wouldn't ask me in for coffee so I threatened that if she didn't I'd kick the milk bottles down the steps. She didn't and I did. Many years later I met a man at the General Synod who told me his two daughters were living in my parish. I didn't know them, so I made a note and called to see them. Two lovely young women, they told me their mother knew me when I was a young fellow and that one night I kicked her milk bottles down the steps!

One night Golding and I went to the Protestant Hall and arrived back to the Harding to find the door locked. We had no late key and the rule was enforced so strictly there wasn't any way to get in. Across the road was the familiar drunken figure who every Friday night after the pubs closed made it his business to stand on the opposite side of the street and shout abuse and obscenities at anyone he saw at the door of the Harding: 'You Protestant bastards are finished. You're auld empire is bunched. You'll all be run out of it yet.'

We had no alternative but to go to York Street, to the Salvation Army Men's Hostel to get a bed for the night. For a shilling the attendant handed us a pillow, sheets and blankets and showed us upstairs to a dormitory of cubicles. Each cubicle had one bed with barely enough room to get in on one side. The floor was bare boards and the light was so dim it was hard to see. There were men fully clothed and in various states of undress, sitting, lying on beds or walking around, some asleep, others talking to themselves. There was a heavy smell of unwashed bodies and booze. We noticed that the ones already in bed had put their shoes under the legs at the head of the bed, and we did the same. We made our beds and got in. I went to sleep eventually to the accompaniment of a cacophony of coughing and hawking and I was careful to put on my shoes before venturing out onto the floor next morning. I made sure I was never locked out of the Harding again.

Neither did I ever go back to the Protestant Hall again. They always ended the night singing 'God Save the Queen,' and I didn't like it – that wasn't where I was coming from.

There was a rule in the Harding that on Sundays all Church of Ireland residents must go to church at St Werburgh's, in Christ Church Place. The rector there was an old man by the name of Canon McPhail. He was a kindly old boy, but he was a poor preacher and he conducted a fairly deadly service. One of the redeeming features, however, of going to St Werburgh's was the young women who also went. Nature dictates that at this age young men and young women will find each other out and where better than at church. None the less this was not enough for me to overcome the deadly dull service, so I used to go in the evenings to St Ann's in Dawson Street. The rector at the time was Archdeacon Sullivan, a great improvement on McPhail, but like the rest of us he had his faults – he had a game leg that he dragged up the aisle in the opening procession. This, however, did not interfere with how well he conducted services of worship. What was more, there was an excellent organist, Willie Watson, and a fine choir. I came to look forward to the Sunday evening service in those days before television when there was a large congregation and good music.

I liked the service at St Ann's, but after it I used to go with other young people to the YMCA Hall in Abbey Street to an evangelical non-denominational service there. It was timed to begin after the evening services in the Protestant churches around the city, and was based on the belief that all of these churches were all right in themselves, but if you hadn't had a conversion experience and given your life to the Lord, as a Christian you weren't the genuine article.

The service was really a hymn, prayer and Bible meeting with an address. As the book of Genesis says, 'male and female he created them'. And so male and female were at the YM on Sunday nights and Mary, in particular, was usually there. The service was constructed carefully to build up to an emotional climax at the end, when the conductor called for people to come forward to the front and publicly give their lives to the Lord. I went to these services for a while but never went forward. One Sunday night during the last verse of the hymn 'Just as I am without one plea' the preacher called for people to come forward. We sang that verse about ten times as he waited for people to make their public profession, and some did, but I saw it for what it was – emotional manipulation – and I never went back. After the service every Sunday evening all the young men and young women walked up Grafton Street where some of them paired off. This was a tradition that had been going on for years. If Mary were there I would walk her home to South Circular Road.

I remember attending the Methodist Centenary Church on St Stephen's Green to hear a well-known evangelical preacher, Alan Redpath. He was a good preacher, but without the emotional manipulation of the preachers at the YM. The religious atmosphere of the Havergal had been quite evangelical as was Archdeacon Waller's parish in Limerick, where we were constantly reminded of the dangers of sin and our need of salvation. The ethos of Miss Carr's Home had been evangelical too, but with a great stress on the love and compassion of God for all people. At this time I was an Old Testament enthusiast. My own Bible reading gave me the sense of God as Father, the Creator who cared for us, his people, as he cared for the Jews in the Old Testament. I can still remember the huge impact the 40th chapter of Isaiah made on me the first time I read it:

'Have you not known? Have you not heard?

The Lord is the everlasting God, the creator of the ends of the earth.

He does not faint or grow weary, his understanding is unsearchable.

He gives power to the faint, and to him who has no might he increases strength.

Even youths shall faint and be weary, and young men shall fall exhausted;

But they who wait for the Lord shall renew their strength,

They shall mount up with wings like eagles,

They shall run and not be weary, they shall walk and not faint.'

While I lived in the Harding, Sunday night service at St Ann's was an important part of my life. I loved the worship, and I loved the music. During my years there I came to know successive curates and without realising it I got a closer view of the work of the ordained ministry.

Canon Daunt succeeded Archdeacon Sullivan and when I left the Harding I went there on Sunday mornings as well as in the evenings and became more involved in the parish. I became a Sunday school teacher, as almost any adult church member could in those days. I taught what I knew, the Bible, and I knew it pretty well from systematic daily reading over the years. It was in St Ann's I got my first taste of amateur dramatics that I will talk about later.

Although I was young I was elected onto the parish select vestry and learned how the Church of Ireland worked. It was not just a matter of learning about the Constitution and the rules that governed procedure, but I learned by watching and listening how people got their point of view across and how some were able to get their own way, in the same way as people do on any kind of committee. Canon Daunt was a shrewd man. He told me that trying to get a vestry to accept change was like going down to the Custom House and trying to demolish it with a tooth pick. He maintained that a rector should confront a select vestry only rarely and then only on important issues. There are times when a rector in a select vestry has to stand up and be counted on matters of principle. I listened and learned a good deal.

During my time on the vestry there was a caretaker in the parish who had been there a few years and resigned to go to another job. Before he left he changed his mind and wrote to the secretary to withdraw his resignation. The secretary brought up the letter at the next vestry meeting. Most of the members were glad the caretaker was leaving as they said he had become lazy and unsatisfactory, and they spoke against allowing him to withdraw his resignation. This was contrary to my sense of justice. I waited and when the chairman was about to put it to a vote I spoke up. I said it was unfair opportunism not to allow this man to withdraw his resignation. It was not the way a Christian body should behave. Anybody is entitled to change his mind. If his work was generally unsatisfactory he should have been called in and told so, given a warning and if his work did not improve then he could be fired. To hold him to his resignation as a way of getting rid of him was indefensible. Immediately someone who hadn't already spoken agreed with me and when the matter was put to a vote the vestry passed, by a large majority, a resolution to allow the caretaker to withdraw his resignation. Years later when he retired the parish gave a party for him. There was a presentation and speeches saying how much he would be missed and there were tears and sadness at his going.

The first time I told anyone I wanted to be a clergyman was at Moyaliffe when Mrs Kemmis asked me what I wanted to be when I grew up, and her response had been 'Oh, that could never be'. Her negative response had little effect on me – I had a dream and she couldn't take that away. During my time in Moyaliffe I day-dreamed a lot about being ordained. I would lie awake in bed at night and think about it, fully sure it was right for me. I would wonder how to go about it and ended up praying and telling God that he would have to help me. Sometimes I thought I would like to be a missionary, but never dwelt on that for long. Looking back this was all a bit unreal. It is impossible to say how or why it was so much with me, and as the circumstances of my life progressed it sometimes took second place to survival and at other times it came back with a bang, stronger than ever. It never left me entirely alone and I would argue with myself about when I was going to do something about it. I have a clear memory, later on, of walking down Harcourt Street on my way to work and arguing with myself that if I didn't make up my mind by my birthday on 14 September I would never do it. So I settled for that and of course my birthday came and went and I did nothing. This kind of thing happened many times until I began to realise that if I didn't try to achieve my goal, one day I would have great regrets.

The pattern for boys living in the Harding was to stay there until they got established in a job and found their way around Dublin and then for three or four to move out into a flat together and have the freedom to come and go as they pleased. This was the route I took and in the spring of 1954, with Golding Kidd who worked in insurance, Dan Swift in the bank and Vivian Dudgeon in the drapery trade, I moved into a flat at 46 Grosvenor Square, Rathmines. The word abroad among some of the others in the Ranch was that we wouldn't stick it a week. As it transpired we were together for almost ten years.

CHAPTER SEVEN

The Mill and The Flat

Life in a flat with three others was a different kettle of fish from life in the Harding. Living at close quarters you had to learn how to respect and tolerate the temperaments and idiosyncrasies of the others and hope they would respect yours. You had to learn how to cope with the banter and how to give and take a ribbing – a ribbing that was often close to the bone and sometimes too close for comfort. I was not very good at coping with this at first and I would rise to the bait quickly. It took me some time to learn that my reaction only provided diversion for the others. Vivian was the worst – baiting me was something of a sport for him until I learned to steel myself to ignore it and even to bait him in return. Over time they all eventually gave up when they saw that I would no longer rise and that I had become skilled at the baiting game myself. It did take me some time, however, before I let the others know something of my background. I didn't tell them the whole story but I gave them the gist of it in dribs and drabs. As friendships grew so did confidences.

Golding and I shared one bedroom and Dan and Vivian shared the other. I had spent more time with Golding than with the others when we were in the Harding. Dan was taciturn, but when he engaged he had a droll wit. He was a congenial flat-mate. Vivian was lively and he was easy to live with too. Each cooked for himself and looked after his own grub, apart from the basics like milk and bread. We kept an account of communal household expenses that we divided between us at the end of the week and we had a rota for washing up and cleaning. Washing up took place usually when there were no more clean dishes and the cleaning was harmless and infrequent. We took it

in turns to be 'on duty,' a week at a time. This meant being responsible for making sure there was a supply of milk, bread,
and shillings for the gas meter, and for putting out the dustbin.
Dan Swift used to say that it was as certain as day follows night
that if there was no milk or no shillings for the meter or the dustbin wasn't put out you knew it was Dalton's week on. I of course
dispute this. He also tells me that I always had an excuse. My account is that if I did occasionally slip up I had good reason!

At first we relished all the freedoms that flat life provided.
Each could cook what he wanted, stay out at night as late as he
liked and lie in bed as long as he felt like at weekends. Within
reason we had our friends to the flat, and if any of us wanted to
bring in a girl we booked the sitting-room in advance and lit a
big fire. The protocol was that nobody else would use the sitting-
room on that night. From time to time we threw a party and for
one party in particular Golding was responsible.

He tidied the place up, made sandwiches and provided
records, and although he invited people for eight o'clock there
was no sign of anyone until the pubs closed. Then the flat was
invaded by a crowd of rowdies carrying brown paper bags of
stout from the pub, led by a fellow we called the Fuhrer, singing
'We're Off to See the Wild West Show'. Golding, who was not a
great drinker himself, was afraid things would get out of hand
and put out one of the particularly truculent new arrivals. He
threatened to put Les Shiel out too if he didn't stop eating the
sandwiches before time, and he wouldn't let the woman who
lent him the cutlery into the party at all because she came late.
He had his own standards of propriety that he found hard to im-
plement on that particular night. In those days I didn't drink
much either, but to preserve my own small supply of booze for
the night I hung it out one of the back windows on a piece of
rope.

Every Sunday night we played poker with some other ex-
Ranchers and their friends who lived in flats nearby. Baiting was
an ancillary pastime to these evenings and my experience with
the other three in our flat helped me to hold my own. This was

before television, and Sunday evening followed a routine. Most of us went down first to the evening service at St Ann's to say our prayers and then back to one of the flats. Jim Parke was a great fan of 'Top Twenty' on Radio Luxemburg so we all had to listen to that. We also listened to 'Community Hymn Singing' on the BBC Light Programme and as soon as that was over the cards were produced and we got down to the serious business of the evening.

I made it a principle to pay all my bills for the week before I decided how much I could afford for poker. It was usually about twenty-five shillings, and consistently for about two years I lost some or all of that every Sunday night. I never seemed to get good cards, and the lads told me it was a learning process! One night there were eleven pokers out, five straights and a royal and I didn't have any of them. Then one Saturday night we all happened to meet in The Red Shoes café in Rathmines and decided to go to one of the flats to play poker. Once again I got terrible cards and we played right through the night until 5 o'clock on Sunday morning and reconvened later in the day. I left the others to it while I went to the evening service in St Ann's on Sunday night. I didn't mention the bad cards to God in my prayers, but when I got back my luck changed and I could do no wrong. However, I got a headache and as the game went on the headache got worse and I almost gave up. The worse the headache got the better the cards became, so I stuck it out and for the first time I made money. Eventually I succumbed to the headache and had to leave the run of good luck behind me and go to bed.

On Saturday afternoons the other three either played rugby or hockey or watched a match of some kind, none of which attracted me. Around this time I began to take an interest in stamp collecting. This had been triggered by a minor find I made at a house auction and it resulted in my continuing my search for stamps some Saturday afternoons. I was also interested in horse racing, studied form and visited Joe Cunningham's to place an occasional bet, but the inside of bookies' offices and their clientele did not appeal to me so I indulged this interest but modestly. Having the flat to myself on Saturday afternoons I used to fill the bath and steep in it reading a book until the hot water ran cold.

There was good camaraderie between us in the flat and there was no shortage of arguments, usually about religion or politics. Sometimes these became hot and heavy but when they were over there were no hard feelings. Outside we would look out for one another but each had his own social life. At one stage the other three were all doing steady lines, so I was left to my own devices and decided that I ought to learn ballroom dancing in order to help with the girls. I enrolled for lessons in a dancing school near the Gaiety Theatre, but I wasn't a natural and found it difficult. As soon as I could make a reasonable attempt at the foxtrot, the quickstep and the slow waltz, I left and took my chances on the dancefloors of Dublin.

There was no shortage of dances around Dublin in those days. Most of us began by going to the Church of Ireland parish 'hops' in Rathfarnham, Sandford, the Molesworth Hall and Clondalkin, where the city met the country. The rectors used to sit near the door to make sure only Protestants went in and in some places you had to sign your name in a book and state which parish you came from. The purpose of this was to avoid mixed marriages and the unjust conditions of the *Ne Temere* decree of the Roman Catholic Church which said that all children of mixed marriages must be brought up as Roman Catholics.

Then there were dances at tennis and rugby clubs and in due course I graduated to public dance halls around the city. I was a regular at the Crystal in Ann Street and went occasionally to the National, where 'culchies', recently arrived in the city, danced. I also went to the Metropole and to Clerys, but my favourite place to dance was the CIE Club in Marlborough Street, where the Royella Swingtette played on Saturday nights. Saturday after Saturday I went there and as I was often short of money I would arrange to meet Kathleen, the current girlfriend, inside. I can still remember the gay abandon with which one New Year's Eve we danced the night away, with not a care in the world.

I had the normal courting instincts of a young man and rapidly fell in and out of love. None of my liaisons lasted long as I suppose that unconsciously I knew that before I became seriously involved with anyone I had to deal with the monkey on my back – the business of becoming a clergyman. We were prepared to go anywhere for a party and for one we were invited to a boat on the Shannon. All four of us decided to go and I was delegated to hire a car from a fellow who rented cars as a sideline. It was a somewhat dilapidated Morris Minor, but with a little coaxing it got us there and back. Petrol was cheap and it wasn't expensive to hire the car. The party was great and a day or so later in the flat we came to settle between us for the evening's expenses. One hell of a row broke out when I told them I had taken the cheapest quote for the car that didn't include insurance. Swift swore he would never get into a car with me again, Kidd was shocked into saying nothing and despite everything Dudgeon was just glad the car hire cost as little as it did. I pleaded innocence as the only way to still the storm, but I must confess I wasn't entirely ignorant of the exact situation.

Jim Parke was one of the regular members of our poker school. He came from Carrickmacross, Co Monaghan, and invited me home with him one weekend. His father ran a pub in Castleblayney and he was well known in the area. On the Saturday night we crossed the border with some friends of Jim's to a dance in Armagh. At the dance they sang Orange and Northern Protestant songs, and the whole atmosphere was one of vitriol and hatred for Roman Catholics and the South of Ireland. I was dumbfounded. I found it hard to believe, as it was the first time I heard anything like it and I never wanted to experience the like of it again. On the way home B Specials stopped us at a roadblock. They stuck a gun in the window and demanded to know who we were and where we were going. I sang dumb and Jim leaned forward from the back seat and said: 'You know Willie Parke of Castleblayney, well I'm his son. We're on our way home from a dance in Armagh.' They withdrew the gun and the whole atmosphere changed and pleasantries were exchanged before we went on our way. The four of us in our flat all came from the South of Ireland where inter religious community relations were formal at this time but mutually respectful between Roman Catholics and Protestants and that night in Armagh was an eye-opener for me.

The flat was in the parish of Rathmines and the others went to church there from time to time. We all came from a church-going background and despite the freedom not to, we all went to church most of the time. Although by this time I was involved in St Ann's, Dawson Street, for some reason or other the four of us always went to Rathmines church on St Patrick's Day. The rector there was Archdeacon Tobias, who had been a chaplain in the First World War. By this time he was elderly and a bit de-crepit. He was lightly built, had silvery hair and a ruddy com-plexion. Once a year he paid a pastoral visit to the four of us in the flat. When the others saw him coming, in order to provoke me they'd say: 'Here's that auld fella' coming again. Don't let him in,' but I could never leave the door closed to a clergyman and I went and let him in. They knew I would. He would come up and sit on the edge of a chair in the kitchen and we'd give him a cigarette. He'd light the cigarette but didn't smoke it. He held it between his fingers and I remember having a side bet as to whether the ash would fall on his suit before he stubbed it. Despite their threat not to let him in, the others were respectful to the old man as we tried to make conversation, while he sat and rambled on about nothing of consequence. After about three quarters of an hour of sometimes excruciating awkward-ness he went, no doubt satisfied he had done his duty for another year.

Working in the Port Mill I came in contact with a broad cross-section of people, from the chairman P. D. Odlum to Ned Kelly who swept the floor. I had little or no sense of status or lack of it either for them or for myself. I took them all as I found them. They took me as I was and I got on well with almost all of them. I had a sense that they were willing to help a lame dog over a stile, and I was a lame dog in that I didn't have a family background or an education that some of them had. Sometimes this played on my mind. I was glad of the support, but I would have been sensitive to being patronised. Nobody did patronise me – in fact on the contrary, I was treated, as far as my work was concerned, like anybody else.

P. D. Odlum was known as 'the big man,' for he was well over six feet tall. He wore a white coat and was likely to turn up anywhere around the mill at any time. The men always knew where he was – they had a kind of bush telegraph system in operation. They kept an eye on him from the time he arrived in his office in the morning and if there was anything in particular going on they would have a lookout posted to watch for him. He was respected rather than liked. One day I was half sitting on a table at the intake point to rest my foot in which I had had osteomyelitis. I saw the big man coming and I knew he had seen me so I saw no point in getting off the table. He came over to talk to me and I stood up. He asked me about the state of the wheat and the work of the intake generally and went off. Later that day Tommy Nixon came and told me Mr Ferguson, the manager, wanted to see me:

'You're in trouble,' he said, 'Mr Odlum has told him to fire you.'

He told me Ferguson was upset and said to him: 'I can't fire the young fellow, he has nobody belonging to him.'

Afraid of my life I went in to see Ferguson. He had an undershot jaw and looked quite fierce when he was cross.

'Kevin,' he said sternly, 'Mr Odlum has told me to dismiss you. He said you were lounging on a table instead of doing your work.'

My heart sank.

'However,' he said, 'I'm not going to fire you this time. I'm going to give you a chance. I'll put you on three weeks' trial and if you don't improve or if I have any complaints about you, you're out. I can't help you if you won't help yourself.'

At this time Mr Ferguson knew me better than Mr Odlum and so he was prepared to stand up for me. This incident put me on my mettle, and I must have improved as I didn't hear another word about it.

As with PD the men always had a fair idea whereabouts around the mill Mr Ferguson was. He was strict about some things, and one of these was smoking. It was an absolute 'no no' to smoke on the premises. He was, of course, right, as a naked light was extremely dangerous where there was wheat dust around. A dust explosion is the most feared thing in the milling business and could blow the whole mill building to kingdom come. A man caught smoking would be sacked on the spot. One day Jock Moyle was sweeping the gantry in an isolated part of the mill, and having a quiet smoke, when 'Fergo' appeared out of nowhere. Jock got such a fright that he swallowed the half-finished cigarette. 'Fergo' came up to him, caught him by the neck and said, 'Spit it out. Spit it out.' Jock stuttered innocently, 'Spit what out, Mr Ferguson?'

Working in the mill there were all kinds and conditions of men and it was important to get on with them all. There was a particular character called Johnny, known to everyone as Scoby. He used to drink with Brendan Behan. He was a difficult man at work and he used the foulest language. I got on well with him, but Tommy Nixon who was in charge of the silo was not always on good terms with Scoby. Now there were big bins a hundred feet deep and to find out how much room was left in them you put a weight on the end of a tape, lowered it down and when the tape went slack, you read the tape and calculated the cubic capacity of the bin. Tommy was measuring one day and dropped the tape into the bin. He called Scoby and told him:

'Go up and get the tape for me, it's in the bin.'

'I will f…ing not.' He says 'I'll have to get danger money for that.'

'There'll be no danger money,' says Tommy. 'Now go up and get the tape or I'll go to Mr Ferguson.'

'You can go to who you f…ing well like,' says Scoby, 'I'm not doing it without danger money.' So Tommy reported Scoby, and Mr Ferguson sent for him, but Scoby had spoken to his shop steward in the meantime and his shop steward went with him to Ferguson. The result was that Scoby got his danger money.

I came on duty on the afternoon shift at noon and heard what had happened. At about half past two I was measuring a bin and didn't I drop the tape. I dreaded telling Scoby, and when I did I said:

'You'll never guess what's happened?'

'You dropped the f…ing tape into the bin.'

'I did,' says I.

'Well f..k you,' he said, but he went up and got it, and not a word about danger money.

The trade unions were strong in those days and the men knew it, but I got on well with Mick Ryan the senior shop steward and we trusted each other. Ned Kelly, the labourer, counted the empty bags after the wheat came out of the wagons and folded them in batches of twenty for re-use. When the wheat was taken off the wagons there would sometimes be a spill of wheat on the road. This was one of Mr Odlum's pet hates and consequently one of Mr Ferguson's too. It was Ned's job to sweep up any spills when the wagons were moved and keep the road clean. One day after we had emptied the wagons I said to Ned:

'Would you ever go out and sweep up, there's a lot of wheat on the road?'

He mumbled to himself and went off. Later on I saw he hadn't done it and I said to him:

'I thought I asked you to sweep up that wheat. Will you go and do it now?' He went off but he still didn't sweep up the wheat.

Later on Mr Ferguson arrived and, calling me out to the hopper intake, he said:

'Look at that wheat on the road. I've spoken to you about that before. Get it swept up at once.' So I called Ned again and asked him to sweep up the wheat. He still didn't do it. He was asked three times, like Peter at the trial of Christ. That very day Mr Odlum arrived down and he was very angry with me when he saw the state of the ground. He told me in no uncertain terms how he thought I was running the intake.

There were wagons due in later that evening which would normally have meant overtime for Ned. But when he asked me if I wanted him that evening I said, 'No, you can go home at 5 o'clock.'

'And whose going to pull down the wagons?'

'Don't you worry about that,' I said. So I pulled down the wagons myself.

Next day when Ned discovered what I had done, he went off and made a formal complaint to the union. Mick Ryan, the shop steward, came down to see me:

'Kevin, Ned Kelly wants me to call the men out over what you did. Did you do it?'

'I did, Mick,' I said.

'You know you broke the rules, why did you do it?'

'Three times I asked the bugger to sweep the road and he wouldn't do it, and he got me into trouble with Mr Odlum and Mr Ferguson.'

'There are procedures for dealing with that. You should have used them. Will you promise you won't do it again?'

'I will,' I said, and he didn't involve the union.

I was content in the mill and I liked the work, and by and large I liked the people I worked with. Around this time there were a number of fellows from good secondary schools coming into the mill. One day after work while PD gave me a lift up to Butt Bridge he asked me, 'Kevin, are you going to do the milling exams, because if you don't you'll be left behind, fellows like Molloy will pass you out?'

A bit like Doonan and the mile race, I didn't like the idea of being passed out, so I asked him what was involved. He told me to ask his cousin Loftus, which I did, and I decided to start the evening classes at Kevin Street tech, with three of the others, in the autumn. It was a discipline for me not to miss these lectures, but PD's 'you'll be left behind' kept me motivated to go to them.

I was now 22 years of age and I hadn't sat in a classroom since I left Limerick five years previously. Evening lectures in

Kevin Street were a far cry from Bifty's class in the Havergal. In addition to the four of us there were eight or nine others from mills around the city. We studied flour milling, flour milling technology and flour milling science. I found most of the topics interesting as many of them related to what I was doing in work, but I found flour milling science more difficult than the others as I had never heard of subjects like physics or biology before. I realised quickly that it was a matter entirely for myself how well I attended and how well I listened at the lectures. Using notes I took in lectures and the prescribed books, I studied two or maybe three nights a week. The flat was quiet enough as none of the others was studying and they were usually out.

We did the Irish milling exams and the exams of the London City and Guilds. Walter de Lacy taught technology and he produced £10 for each of us from the Irish Flour Millers Association when we passed the exams. Bob Darcy, the cereal chemist from the Port Mill, lectured us in science and he was brilliant. He was a natural teacher. He had the gift of not only making things clear but of making them interesting. I met someone only recently, a cereal chemist too, who said that Bob in his day was one of the most respected cereal chemists in Europe.

Competition, they say, is the soul of trade, and it was also the motivation for me not only to pass but also to do well in the exams. I was determined to do better than the others, and got 1st class honours in the two London City and Guilds exams and came first in Ireland on two occasions in the Irish exams. Despite the recurrent niggle about becoming a clergyman, I was determined to qualify as a miller in order to have something to fall back on in case I failed in the ordination stakes, so when I qualified it gave me a new kind of confidence, and brought to the surface again my objective of getting into Trinity to study Divinity. I could no longer make the excuse to myself that I wouldn't be able to pass exams to get into college. I remember telling myself a number of times that if I ever reached the biblical three score years and ten and had not made the effort, I would be an old man full of regrets. I knew deep down that at least I would have to try, even if I failed. I remember reminding myself that I didn't want to end up when I was 70 regretting that I hadn't tried.

I struggled, however, with the internal conflict that I kept entirely to myself. I was doing well at work; I had a good wage and I had become experienced at determining the quality of Irish wheat. I valued this financial freedom and the satisfaction of my job. There was another complicating factor – I had been doing an on-and-off line with Kathleen, one of the girls at work.

There was a recognised short non-graduate course in biblical studies for older men that led to ordination in the Church of Ireland, but I didn't want to apply for that since I was sure they wouldn't accept someone with my lack of secondary education. I was determined either to do the full five-year graduate course for ordination or stick with milling. It became clear to me that if I was to try for ordination the right thing for me to do was to study for Trinity entrance exam which would not only gain me entrance, but the work itself would make up something of what I had missed of secondary education. Furthermore I had a bit of a stubborn streak that made me feel that when I was ordained I didn't want to have done it the easy way.

Eventually I came to the conclusion that there was no way out. I would have to try for ordination. By this time I was friendly with another girl called Helen whom I had met at one of the parish dances, so I decided to tell her my plan to go to Trinity to study for ordination. It was a ruse of mine because I knew when I told her I could not back down and I hoped she wouldn't keep it to herself and would tell others, making it even harder for me to duck the issue any longer. The strategy worked. Once others knew it was a spur to me to go ahead and to succeed. I went to P. D. Odlum and told him I was going to try for matriculation and why. Despite the fact that he was sick and tired of his trainee millers moving off elsewhere when they qualified, he wished me well and said, 'Kevin, I'll help you any way I can,' and he meant it.

I got hold of the course syllabus and chose what I thought were my five most likely subjects within the constraints of the requirements. As an avid reader of the daily newspapers and of *Time* and *Newsweek* magazines I had a great interest in world affairs. This coupled with the fact that I had always done well at history and geography in the Havergal made me choose both those subjects. I chose physics as a subject I would have to start from the beginning, and English was compulsory. One or other of Latin or maths was also compulsory. I knew that there was no way on God's earth that I could get maths so I was left with Latin, another subject I would start from the beginning.

Before setting into these subjects for Trinity entrance I decided to take a correspondence course in English, history and geography. Two women I knew, Amy Phillips, a teacher, and Dorothea Waller, a retired missionary and a grandniece of Archdeacon Waller, helped me with the work of the correspondence course. The only thing I remember about that course was an essay I wrote entitled 'An Autumn Day'. With the avenue of Moyaliffe in mind on an autumn evening I wrote:

'Underneath my feet was a carpet of dead brown leaves. It reminded me that even as the day was sinking so was the year and even as the year was sinking so too was one's own span of life. And as I thought on this I hoped my departure would be as peaceful as this.'

When the course tutor returned the essay he had written on it: 'Is this your own work or did you poach it from someone?'

I found this remark offensive, as it was all my own work, so I chose to ignore it. I also bought a Longmans Latin Grammar and proceeded to try and teach myself, learning the declensions off by heart and then trying to do the exercises, but with no great success. The exam was in October and in the evenings over the summer I studied hard after my day's work. The other lads in the flat were tolerant of 'the bishop's' need for extra quiet over the summer.

In order to earn extra money I would need when I entered Trinity in October, I took off from study the two weeks of my summer holidays and went with a friend, Paddy from the mill, to work on a Bord na Móna bog in Lanesboro, Co Longford. It was tough work, but good fun. For the first week there was a group of five of us footing turf, which is no joke of a job for beginners. One member of the group was a teacher from Marlborough Street and to say that he was indolent would be to flatter him. While the rest of us were working he would sit in the sun on the ditch and regale us with stories of his pupils in the inner city. As soon as he spotted the foreman he would jump up, give the appearance of industry and engage the foreman in a technical conversation about the composition and quality of the turf.

On Sunday Paddy and the indolent teacher, both Roman Catholics, and I went to church at the local Church of Ireland church. There were so few there the rector was delighted to see us and invited us back to the rectory after the service for sherry. The other two sang dumb about their religious allegiance and knocked back the sherry to the extent that our unfortunate host had to open another bottle into which we made good inroads before we left. For the second week I got away from the footing and fed one of the conveyor-belts, which was only marginally easier work but longer hours. The money, however, was good and my net profit for the two weeks was £30, a considerable sum for me in those days.

In October I sat the exam and when I heard the results were out I called in to Trinity on my way home from work. I was not surprised to find that I had passed history, geography and English, and failed physics and Latin. At this time it was possible to hold three subjects you passed so I had three under my belt. By now it was clear to me that I would never pass physics, so for the next exam I changed to biology and of course I had no option but to repeat Latin. My milling exams were a great help with biology and I don't know why I didn't choose it in the first place, so next time out I passed biology and failed Latin again. I knew I would need help with Latin so Jim O'Donoghue, the chemist from Procea, helped me. He was an accomplished linguist. He would set me exercises to do from Longmans Latin Grammar and I'd bring them over at lunchtime for him to correct. I found the Latin hard and I failed it again. That was three times. I couldn't help feeling they were putting up the standard every time I sat it and they were keeping just ahead of me. I have to thank O'Donoghue for keeping me to it. When I was despondent he would tweak my conscience and challenge me to do something about it. When PD knew results were due he would ask me how I got on and once when I told him I had failed, he put his arm around my shoulder and said: 'When are you sitting it again?'

Canon Daunt, the rector of St Ann's, to whom I had told my story, supported me too. At one stage he took the trouble to go down to see P. D. Odlum, though I never knew what transpired between them, but I have no doubt the visit contributed towards PD's encouragement to me. One of the times I failed Latin I was particularly despondent and talking to Canon Daunt he said to me, 'If you're so determined to be ordained you could go to the London Bible College to train.' I didn't entertain the idea as I suspected the kind of theology I would study there would be the evangelical kind so beloved of Williams, my first employer in Dublin. He would have been pleased to hear if I had gone there, in fact I have no doubt he would even have financed me.

With the help of Jim O'Donoghue, my Latin tutor from the lab, the moral support of P. D. Odlum, my other friends and my own determination in my better moments, after nine attempts – three a year for three years – I eventually passed Latin and qualified to enter Trinity.

As soon as I had passed the matriculation examination Canon Daunt advised me to make an appointment to see the Archbishop, George Simms. The authority figures in my life to date had been diverse – Miss Carr, gentle and caring; Archdeacon Waller, authoritarian; Mickey with the chair leg and Bifty the brute with his stick and vicious tongue; Jess Kemmis, who always got her own way and the honourable Captain; Ferguson with the hard exterior and the soft heart, and the supportive and encouraging P. D. Odlum. I was about to meet another one in the person of George Otto Simms. I rang the doorbell of the See House on Marlborough Road and thought to myself, 'He may be an archbishop but he's still human like the rest of us. Don't worry about him.'

I needn't have worried. He was a most kind and gracious man who put me at my ease. I told him my story and how since I was a small boy I wanted to be ordained and that I had recently passed Trinity matric. We got involved in a discussion about St Paul and I think he was mildly impressed by my knowledge of the Bible. He did, however, gently suggest that I might attend Holy Communion more often. He then explained to me the procedure followed in the Church of Ireland for those wishing to be ordained. I would have to attend a three-day selection conference designed to assess the suitability of candidates for ordination. 'Of course,' he said, 'nobody can say for certain that you have or haven't got a vocation. Only God knows that. We have, however, found it a helpful method in deciding who should be ordained.' When I was leaving he gave me a book, *People Matter More Than Things*, and those words, in my experience over the years spoke to me of the essence of the man.

As a result of this interview I went to a residential three-day selection conference. At the conference five assessors interviewed each candidate from different aspects of what vocation involved: academic, psychological, social, church commitment and spirituality. The other dozen or so candidates there were of a variety of ages and came from different parts of the Church of Ireland, North and South.

In my interview with Archdeacon Quin, one of the assessors, he asked me if I were a rector in a parish and went into a house for the first time how would I break the ice. I told him I'd say, 'Howya?' I was not impressed with the conference or the assessors. I had a feeling they were feeling their way, but I was conscious that they had my future in their hands as far as serving in the ministry of the Church of Ireland was concerned.

Shortly after the conference the archbishop asked to see me and told me I had been recommended for training. I was greatly relieved and excited that at last I was about to begin. He asked me how I enjoyed the experience of the conference so I told him what I thought. Then he said:

'And Kevin, what kind of questions did they ask you?'

'One fellow asked me if I had ever been drunk?'

He smiled broadly and asked:

'And what was your reply?'

I told him it depended on what he meant by 'drunk.' Like most things, apart from death, there are degrees.

'Any other questions?'

'One of the examiners asked some of the candidates if they'd ever known a woman they would like to sleep with.' No comment from the archbishop, so I continued: 'If he'd asked me I'd have said yes.' The archbishop just smiled.

I continued to work in the mill until the Friday before I started in Trinity. I had mixed feelings about leaving. I had worked there for nine years and the many friends I made had been good to me. My usual morning routine for years had been that since I got up too late to have time for breakfast, when I arrived in work I went over to the girls in the canteen to have a mug of tea. My last morning was no different and when I went across to the canteen all the girls were there. They had a place laid for me with a tea towel at one of the tables. Set out on it were a boiled egg, some toast and a pot of tea. When I finished my breakfast Sadie Ryan spoke for them all and said how much they would miss me and they wished me well in college. Then they presented me with an inscribed watch, which I have to this day. I enjoyed the fuss the girls made of me. Peter Odlum told me that in his memory in the mill it was the first time that the workers had made a presentation to a member of staff.

CHAPTER EIGHT

Trinity

For three years I had spent more than my share of time going into Trinity to view the notice-board outside the exam hall for entrance exam results, especially failed Latin ones, but on those occasions I didn't venture further. Despite early over-confidence I did not want to anticipate what was problematic. When I entered Trinity it was a foreign world to me. None the less, on my first day I was excited. I had an immense sense of achievement, but I was conscious that I was nine or ten years older than most of my fellow students. I was defensive because I saw the other students as privileged – family-wise, socially, educationally and financially – but as usual when I felt like this it brought out in me a determination that served to spur me on to achieve my goal and not to allow anyone to intimidate me.

On that first day I stood on the steps outside the examination theatre and surveyed the students in Front Square coming and going, and students standing in groups around the society stalls touting for new members from among the junior freshmen. It was one of the most important days of my life. I knew that my efforts in the past had been worthwhile, and that I was now firmly facing in the right direction. I was on the road that for years I believed was right for me. Trinity was a privileged island in the centre of the city in which I had lived and worked for ten years. From reading history I was aware of its traditions and of the many illustrious people who were its graduates. As I stood there I resolved that whatever the next five years might bring I would keep my friends in the flat and the mill, and that any friendships I might make in college would not supplant them.

In the first week I had to see my tutor and I met outside his door, also waiting to go in, another prospective ordinand, Fred Graham, from the North of Ireland. I gauged him to be near to my own age. I suggested that after the interviews we might go for a cup of coffee. He was diffident and replied, 'I don't know about that,' and he wouldn't agree to meet me. I was hurt and thought to myself, 'So that's what they are like in here. Well he can go to hell.' I was taken aback by his caution, but on reflection I realised that as a Northerner he would be naturally cautious and that he was probably feeling a bit vulnerable too. Afterwards we became particularly good friends.

By now we had moved flat from Grosvenor Square to 22 Castlewood Avenue, Rathmines. Golding and Vivian were married and John Craig and Sam Mehaffey replaced them. Until my final two years, when I was required to live in the Divinity Hostel, I lived in the flat and kept my place there even when I was in the Hostel. The flat was the only place that was my own.

Financially I was sailing close to the wind. I had to go on paying my way in the flat and I had to buy books and provide all the appurtenances of college life. Trinity was very good to me. When I declared my financial situation they reduced my fees to almost nil, and gave me some small bursaries. As an intending ordinand the Church of Ireland gave me a grant, but I was still short of the minimum I needed to live. Some of the lads I knew from the Harding worked in the Royal Bank, so I went up to the branch in Grafton Street to ask for an overdraft, and offered them a small life insurance policy as security. To my amazement they gave me an overdraft of £350 which would see me through my first college year, and that was as far ahead as I was prepared to think for the moment.

For my degree subjects I chose history, philosophy and Hebrew. History I liked and it was never any trouble to me. Philosophy, which included logic, was new to me, but I realised dimly that people like Descartes and Hume, who were mentioned in the syllabus, were part of something I had only a vague idea about called the Enlightenment, that had an influence on the way we thought about ourselves. I chose Hebrew since I had eventually passed Latin and I believed it would not be impossible for me to handle another language, especially when everybody taking it would be starting from the beginning. I was further attracted to it as it was the original language of my beloved Old Testament. My knowledge of the Old Testament of the Authorised Version of the Bible helped me out of many a spot with unseen translations in subsequent exams.

At the end of my first year the Hebrew lecturer, Canon Tom Salmon invited me one day for coffee. He was a saintly man and wanted me to transfer to honours Hebrew. He said it was my duty to prepare myself to the best of my ability for the service of Jesus Christ and his church. I was flattered and gave the matter some thought. Exams for pass Hebrew were held in June, which would allow me to work during the summer to earn money towards the following year. If I took honours, since the honours exams were in October, I would have to study over the summer and I would not be able to work. This decided the matter for me, and when I explained to him the world in which I lived, Tom understood and accepted my reason for declining his suggestion to change to honours Hebrew.

Around this time more and more students had access to university. Trinity, in common with other universities, found that many students highly qualified to enter were defective in their written English. To address this problem the College required every new entrant in their first term to write an English essay under exam conditions. You could have three attempts and if you didn't pass you were out on your ear. There were to be no semi-literate graduates of TCD. When I learned of this requirement my heart sank, for given the paucity of my early education, despite a correspondence course in the meantime, I knew my written English was bad. I knew there was a real danger I might not get over this hurdle.

I sat the essay for the first time and went to have it returned by the examiner, Dr Gerald Simms, an historian and brother of Archbishop Simms. I hoped that Gerald Simms would have the same kind and understanding disposition his brother had. I entered his room and he indicated to me to sit down. There were no preliminaries. 'Dalton,' he said. 'I don't think I have ever read, or tried to read, an essay that had as little proper English in it. You can't write, you can't spell and your grammar is appalling. I'm going to fail you.' It shook me, but I knew in my heart he was right. I did think, however, he could have let me down a little more gently.

Before I was due to sit the essay for the second time I went a number of times to Amy Phillips to get help with grammar, punctuation and spelling. She did her best but I knew I hadn't made much progress. For my second attempt I chose from the list of topics the subject 'Katanga'. As an avid reader of current affairs I was well informed on the secession of Katanga from the newly independent Belgian Congo. I wrote a long essay about the history and development of Katanga and its current problems. When the time came to have the essay returned I went to the examiner, Vincent Denard, to collect it. His serious face looked ominous to me and my hope drained swiftly away. I sat down. 'Dalton,' he said, 'your grammar is terrible, your spelling is worse, but I have seldom read such an informative essay. Despite some difficulties in reading it, I enjoyed it and I'm going to pass you.' I couldn't believe it. I had survived again.

In junior freshman year all prospective ordinands were obliged to attend catechetical lectures on Saturday mornings. This was to ensure that they had a basic knowledge of the Bible before embarking on the study of divinity. For one term the Regius Professor of Divinity, The Reverend Canon Richard Hartford, gave these lectures. He was a man with a great awareness of his own importance. His wife was the daughter of the former Archbishop of Dublin. The clergy used to say that the only reason he married the Archbishop of Dublin's daughter was that the Archbishop of Canterbury hadn't got a daughter. One Saturday morning he began his lecture by saying, 'I want all my students in College Chapel to morrow morning because I'm preaching,' and a voice from the back of the class added, 'and I'm good.'

Hartford had a lisp and he was quite a wit. One morning he expressed the hope that all his students read the daily papers. 'If you read *The Irish Times* this morning you'd have noticed an interesting thing. There was an article about an alleged saint called St Philomena. The Pope has now declared that she never existed. A predecessor of mine as Regius Professor wrote a book eighty years ago called *The Infallibility of the Church* in which he said there was no such person as St Philomena. This just goes to show that what the Regius Professor of Divinity of Trinity College, Dublin says today the Pope will say tomorrow.'

Another term the catechetical lecturer was Canon Salmon. He lectured on St Luke's gospel. It was the only time I read every book on the course. He was thorough and meticulous and a good teacher if you had the patience to listen to him. When Canon Daunt went to Cork as Dean, Canon Salmon succeeded him as vicar of St Ann's. While I was in Trinity he gave me grinds in Hebrew from time to time in the vestry of St Ann's, especially coming up to exams. In fact he couldn't do enough to help me and when he learned I was living in a flat he invited me to lunch every Sunday with him and his sister Gertie. He was yet another person who helped me on the way.

Financially I was on a tight budget. In the first Christmas vacation I worked in the Post Office sorting mail and in May I skipped lectures and got a couple of days' work at the Spring Show attaching numbers to bulls and to an assortment of other animals. I knew I would have to get work to earn some serious money during the summer vacation if I were to survive in college. At the end of my first year I wrote to the Church of Ireland grants committee and told them I was skint and unless they increased my grant of £100 I might have to consider ordination in another province of the Anglican Communion. They gave me an extra £20!

Most students who worked during the summer went to England and earned £20 a week canning peas or picking fruit. £20 a week was a lot of money for a student in those days. I went to see P. D. Odlum to ask if he could give me a job over the sum-

mer. He was prepared to employ me for £12 a week, so I told
him I could earn £20 in England and declined his offer. Shortly
after I had seen PD I was at a church meeting on mission at the
Metropolitan Hall in Abbey Street and met Alleyn Harris, manager of Waterford Flour Mills, part of the Odlum Group of companies. 'You're the very man I wanted to see,' he said. 'Will you
meet me for lunch tomorrow?' 'Great,' I thought, as only seldom
had anyone bought me lunch before, and knowing Alleyn
Harris it would be a good one. We met for lunch the following
day and he took a great interest in what I was doing and how I
was managing. Then he got down to business:

'I need someone to look after my wheat for the coming season. I have nobody. You have plenty of experience. You're the
very man. Will you come down and do it for me?'

'I will,' I said, 'if you'll pay me £20 a week.'

'I'll have to talk to PD about that.'

'Well do, because I can earn that in England.'

Harris talked to Odlum who agreed to pay the £20 a week, but
he would only let Harris pay me £10 a week and put the other £10
away and give it to me in the autumn when I left to go back to
college. He was right, of course, as if I had access to all of it I
would probably have had very little left by the time term started.

The work in Waterford was not easy as it turned out to be a
bad year for Irish wheat. When I climbed up on the lorries to ex-
amine the grain I found that only a small portion of it was good.
In deciding what was millable and what was unmillable, it
seemed to me that most of it was borderline, and I was conscious
that the livelihood of farmers could depend on my decisions. As
the queue of lorries grew longer and the waiting farmers grew
more anxious I remember talking to myself: 'Look Dalton, you
know very well what's millable and what's not. You know what
you've got to do – reject the stuff that's unmillable, so get on
with it.' This wasn't easy in a year that a high proportion of the
crop was not millable. I made it my business to leave Waterford
at the weekends, as it was easier to deal with agents and farmers
if I didn't meet them socially.

So after the long vacation at the end of my first year in college, having lived in Waterford and having bought the wheat for Alleyn Harris, I went back to college, thanks to P. D. Odlum, with a nest egg that would help to see me through the academic year. For each of the next three years I spent my summers working for the mill, which suited me perfectly because preparations for the wheat season started in June, just when I had finished exams. The season itself began in August and went on into the third week in October when term started again. So I worked some of June, July, August, September and most of October – all grist to my own financial mill.

The second summer Mr Ferguson sent for me and told me there was a problem in the New Ross depot and some wheat had been damaged: 'Will you go down and look after the wheat season in the South East and I'll send Terry Cronin with you?'

The mill hired a car for me and the first thing we had to do was set up and stock two laboratories, one in Wexford and one in Carlow. Then we made contact with the different agents in the region in time for the harvest.

The following year I put it to Mr Milliken that if the mill bought a car for me I could pay it off out of expenses and have the use of it for the rest of the year. Milliken said he'd have to ask Mr Odlum. PD agreed and told Milliken that he would pay for the car himself so that if it didn't work out the company would not be at a loss. So I bought a second-hand powder blue Morris 1000, Leitrim registered, IT 4580.

I bought the car on the Friday of the August bank holiday. It was my pride and joy. On the Monday morning I went out to discover it was gone. I couldn't believe it. Someone had stolen it. I reported it to the Guards and waited. About an hour later I had a phone call from the Guards to say they had found the car about half a mile away. The thieves had abandoned it when it ran out of petrol. My penury had been my good fortune.

For three years that little blue car carried me all around the city in winter and all around the country in summer and never let me down. The first winter I had it there was a particularly heavy fall of snow. It was parked in a side street and another car skidded into it and damaged it badly. The other driver's insurance company admitted liability but they were slow to settle. The problem was that the repairers wouldn't release the car to me until I paid them, so I went to see P. D. Odlum to ask if he would fund me until the insurance company paid up. He put his hand in his pocket, took out his chequebook and asked me how much it was. I told him £375. He handed me the cheque and said, 'Kevin, this is a gift. I never lend money to my friends.' When the insurance company paid up I was in funds as I had never been before.

I have always regretted that I did not take academic work more seriously when I was in Trinity. There were many opportunities, but I lacked the discipline, a commodity I have always been short of, to take full advantage of them. University was for me rather a means to an end, ordination, that end that had haunted and driven me since it first assailed me as a young boy.

In 1960, while I was still in the mill, there was an acute international refugee problem, so much so that the year was designated 'World Refugee Year' by the UN. Aid agencies were appealing for money, but things were tight for most people, so I came up with the idea of putting on a play to raise money. I read a few plays including *Sive* by a new Irish playwright from Kerry, John B. Keane. I liked the story, I liked the language and I knew it would be easy to stage as far as costume and props were concerned. I discussed it with a few of my poker-playing friends and some others, and asked those who were interested to come for an audition. I selected a cast and started rehearsals in the sitting-room of Castlewood Avenue. We were a disparate bunch of individuals, most of us without any acting experience. I had neither acted nor produced before. At first the cast treated the whole thing as a bit of a joke and I had to get cross with them. On one occasion when there was so much laughing and giggling, to the extent that we couldn't go on, I simply walked out and left them. When the hard graft of rehearsal came it was sometimes difficult to get them to rehearsals when I wanted them. I had to be firm and eventually we got to the point of no return. We were on course for a production and towards the end, to give them their due, the cast put in the hard work.

I used my contacts in St Ann's and the parish gave us the use of the Molesworth Hall free of charge. I recruited and sometimes dragooned people for behind-the-scenes and for front-of-house. I was organiser, producer, director and business manager who arranged everything and delegated some of it. For props I told members of the cast that came from the country to bring back oil lamps, wellington boots, three legged pots, holy pictures and pictures of popes. Since the cast was almost entirely Protestant, however, I had to get most of the pictures from friends in the mill. Everybody involved sold tickets, at work and to their friends, and my colleagues at the mill gave me great support.

After a terrible dress rehearsal when I thought the whole thing would be a disaster, the following night we went on. With a few minor hitches and some missed cues it went well. The four nights were a sell out and the whole thing was a great success. Despite the strain and anxiety everybody enjoyed themselves. It had been great fun and very satisfying to do. In addition to everything else I played the part of the lover and the one line that sticks in my mind because it didn't quite fit for a fellow who was planning to be ordained was, 'Go way, go way you horrible filthy bitch that the hand of God may strike you dead where you stand. You heartless wretch that drove poor little Sive to her grave.' We cleared £100, which was a lot of money in those days and I still have the letter of acknowledgement from the Red Cross.

One night, a week or two afterwards, we all met at the flat to see where we might go from here. There was absolute uproar. The women objected to the dictatorial attitude of the director and he would have to go. They demolished me, and of course they were right, but somebody had to do it or the whole thing would never have happened. I knew that some of the cast were resentful of my businesslike approach but I hadn't been aware of the depth of their feelings. The rebels were women who were either courting or engaged, so I decided to sing dumb and wait a couple of years before I put on another play. This is what I did and the next production of The Castlewood Players in aid of famine relief was Keane's *Sharon's Grave*, by which time the rebellious women were married and gone and I was in Trinity.

This time round again it was an *ad hoc* group consisting of some originals from *Sive* and student friends from Trinity. I decided that the only way to get the thing done was for me to run the show again and despite the rebellion last time I was prepared to get cross again when necessary. One of the advantages of putting on Keane was that we could all provide our own costumes from cast-off clothes and the sets were simple. I had the sets for *Sive* made in the mill and had stored them away in the hall and we used them again. We rehearsed in the flat and I had the same unseemly levity and worse to deal with and I employed the same tactics as before – on more than one occasion I told them if they weren't going to take it seriously they could all go home. Sometimes I found it hard to keep a straight face myself, but it had to be done. One night we had to stop altogether when in the wake scene Cecil Elliott spent his time trying to make the corpse laugh and further hilarious complications arose as one of the Catholic members of the cast tried to teach Cecil, the son of a Methodist minister, how to make the sign of the cross.

As with *Sive* we put *Sharon's Grave* on for four nights and it was a sell out every night. Brendan Kennelly, whom I knew from Trinity, came on the first night and told John B Keane about these divinity students who were staging *Sharon's Grave*. Kennelly told me that Keane was coming up from Listowel specially for the production and would be there on the last night. Now at this time John B. could be a bit obstreperous if he didn't like how his work was staged, so on the last night I had a couple of big fellows detailed that if he opened his mouth from the audience they were to put him out. Kennelly told me that Keane would not want to be called on stage at the end. When, however, the final curtain was drawn John B. came forward, stuck his head around the curtain and said: 'Jesus, you're a great crowd o' hoors.' He invited us all down to the Ormond Hotel where he was staying and bought drink to beat the band. He entertained us with talk and song and after about an hour or so he and his wife disappeared to bed without a word and left us to our own devices.

At this time Brendan Kennelly was a junior lecturer in the English Department in Trinity and little known outside the College. He was brimming with life and ideas and he was the best of company. One night he came out for a few drinks with a couple of us. He came back to stay the night with me in the flat and we talked into the small hours of the morning. Amongst other things we inevitably talked religion. I thought 'the dimpled genius from Ballylongford,' as John B. Keane used to call him, would burst with laughter when I told him he was nothing but a backward Kerry Papist.

The following year we put on another Keane play, *The Highest House on the Mountain*. Our reputation was good so we had a loyal following of patrons that meant we sent a third healthy cheque away for world hunger.

The College Theological Society was the extra curricular activity in Trinity that absorbed most of my time. It was a paper-reading rather than a debating society. Meetings were held on Monday nights during term when all kinds of Christian theological issues were aired. I also joined the Historical Society and occasionally attended their debates. There was one in particular when the motion was ' Religion is Bunkum,' a typically provocative student debating motion. A few of us from the 'Theo' felt we couldn't let this pass without having our say, so we went to the debate in what was considered in college the superior society, whose membership largely represented the secular face of the student body. Most of the negative aspects of religion, especially Christianity's attempts to destroy indigenous cultures by missionary activity, were paraded before a full house. On the other side the case was made that, despite all the negatives, where there was suffering and starvation in the world, there too was the cross, there too the voice of Christ could be heard calling to his followers to help.

Despite its small membership the 'Theo' was recognised as a major society in college. This was a hangover from the days, long gone, when the Church of Ireland was a significant influence in the life of the College and Fellows of the College had to be Anglican divines. By this time almost all, if not in fact all, ordinary members of the Theological Society were Church of Ireland ordinands. The rules of the Society stipulated that membership be exclusively Anglican. I, and many others, considered that to be anachronistic and I led a movement that set about changing it. Not only did we want to encourage people who were not ordinands to join, but we also wanted to change the rules to open membership to students of all religions and of none. It should be remembered that in those years every Ash Wednesday *The Irish Times* carried the Lenten Pastorals of the Roman Catholic bishops warning their people of the danger to their immortal souls should they attend Trinity, and forbidding them, on pain of mortal sin, from doing so.

There was formidable opposition within the society, led by John Neill, now Archbishop of Dublin, to any move to change the membership rule. He insisted that membership should remain exclusively Anglican, while there were some, inevitably, who were prepared to open membership to non-conformists, but not to Roman Catholics. After much manoeuvring, manipulating and politicking we won the day and brought the College Theological Society kicking and screaming into the twentieth century when we had the rules changed so that religion was not a criterion for membership. Women, however, according to the rules were still excluded from membership. On one famous occasion Frances Jane French and Stella L'Estrange staged a sit-in before a meeting when the auditor sent for one of the officers of the college. They left under protest when he arrived, and not long afterwards we changed the rules to admit women to membership.

The 'Theo' had its own reading room in college, used almost

exclusively by Church of Ireland ordinands, many of whom were from the North of Ireland, and unionist to a man. I had great sport taunting them. As they sat quietly reading their papers I would put my head around the door and tell them: 'The glory days of the Empire are gone. England will sell Ulster down the river when it suits her, the way she sold out all her other colonies. Face reality and join the Republic before you're forced into it.' This was in the early 1960s. There would be uproar for a while and I'd go off for coffee with someone and when we came back they'd still be at it and I'd throw in a few more provocative comments to keep it going.

In my fourth year in college I was elected auditor of the Theological Society. As a major society the inaugural meeting was a big event. It was held in Michaelmas Term in the Dining Hall with full evening dress for officers and distinguished visitors. The meeting took the form of a paper read by the new auditor who invited four guests to speak to it. I chose as my subject Christian communication, and entitled the paper 'The Oracles are Dumb,' sub-titled 'The Breakdown of Communication between the Church and the World.' It seemed to me that some of the ways the church used to communicate the gospel were becoming obsolete in the modern world.

My first choice as guest speaker was head of religious broadcasting at ITV. The second was a professor of communications at Keele University. The third a retired Anglican Bishop of New Delhi, and the fourth was Brendan Kennelly. I knew that no matter how the others turned out Brendan would be his usual cheerful enthusiastic self and have something worthwhile to say. One Ascension Thursday I met him crossing Front Square and asked him what he thought of this Ascension business. 'A good exit line,' he replied without thinking.

I arranged and confirmed everything for the inaugural by the end of June and went off to work for the summer. One Saturday in mid-September, back in Dublin for the weekend from Wexford where I was buying wheat, I got a letter from the ITV broadcaster to say that he had double booked and he was sorry

he would not be able to come to the inaugural in October. The
next day I read in the *Observer* about a certain American
Anglican bishop, James Pike, who was coming to Cambridge on
sabbatical. He had been a Roman Catholic seminarian as a
young man, but had left and became a successful lawyer. He
subsequently entered an Anglican seminary and was ordained.
In due course he became Dean of the Cathedral of St John the
Divine, New York, and then Bishop of California. Along the way
he had been tried for heresy a couple of times but found not
guilty. He was still bishop and in good standing. There was a
telephone operators' strike on at the time, so on the Monday I
went into the American Embassy and in an American telephone
directory I found his office number in San Francisco. Eventually
I got through to his office where they told me he had already left
for Cambridge and they gave me a number where I could phone
him *en route* in New York. I phoned him there from Wexford and
told him who I was and what I wanted. Without hesitation he
said, 'Mr Dalton, I'd be greatly honoured.'

When I recounted all of this to Don McClatchie, a friend in
my year, he told me I had better go and see George Simms immediately as I had no right to bring a bishop to speak in his diocese without his permission. I was never good on procedures. I
made an appointment and went to see Simms. 'I'm thinking of
inviting Bishop Pike of California to speak to my inaugural
paper,' and explained how the ITV man had let me down. 'I
wonder what your reaction would be?' 'Well Kevin,' he said, 'he
has been cleared.' That was all he said.

Simms was master of the oblique comment. When I was ordained I was in his diocese. At the time Jack Lynch, having
sacked three of his ministers over the importation of arms and
another having resigned, was under severe pressure in Fianna
Fáil so I decided to join my local Cumann and support him at
branch level. I thought I ought to tell Simms as a matter of courtesy. So I told him I was thinking of joining a political party and I
wondered what his reaction would be. 'Well,' he said, 'Kevin,
there's no law against it; it's not the normal thing for clergy, but

there's no law against it.' 'I wonder how you'd feel if I told you the party I was thinking of joining was Fianna Fáil?' He stood looking out the window for what seemed an age, and turned to me and said: 'I think it would be unreasonable for anyone to suggest that Fianna Fáil has a monopoly on original sin.'

A couple of years later when Alan Buchanan was Archbishop of Dublin, Simms having gone to Armagh, I was on holiday in Donegal. There was an election at the time and I bumped into Des Hanafin, who was director of elections. 'You're a member of the party,' said he to me. 'I am,' said I. 'Will you do some canvassing?' said he. 'I will,' said I. So he sent me out to an area where there was a traditional Protestant vote that Fianna Fáil lost last time out in a row over a hospital. He asked me to wear my collar but I refused. He phoned up the Fianna Fáil organiser in the area to say I was coming. Hanafin recounted later that when he told the local organiser who I was he said; 'Jesus!' 'No,' replied Hanafin, 'one of his disciples.' I canvassed for a couple of days and at the election Fianna Fáil regained 80% of their lost vote in the area. They won back the seat and the Protestant opposition candidate was defeated.

There was, however, a sequel. Back in Dublin a week or so later I had a call from Dean Salmon, who was in charge of the diocese while Archbishop Buchanan was away in India praying for church unity. When I went to see him he told me he had had a letter from the Bishop of Derry fulminating about the irresponsible behaviour of a young cleric from Dublin who had been at large in his diocese canvassing for Fianna Fáil. Salmon asked, 'Did you tell the local rector you were canvassing in his parish?' 'No,' I said. 'Well perhaps you might write to him and apologise for not paying him that courtesy,' he said in his own quiet and kindly way, 'and I will reply to the bishop.'

I wrote to the rector and apologised for my discourtesy. Salmon showed me his letter to the bishop in which he refuted the bishop's allegations against me, and that was the end of the matter.

To return to the inaugural. A week or so before the event The

Rev Professor A. A. Luce stopped me in Front Square. As a young man he had been in the First World War and was awarded the MC. Now retired, he had been Professor of Metaphysics and a distinguished Berkleyan scholar of international repute. He was a Fellow of the College and Vice-Provost of the University. 'Dalton, I got your invitation to the inaugural and I'm going to come. I don't know where you got the title for your paper. I know I know it, but I cannot recall from where it comes. Where is it from?' I felt ten feet tall. 'From Milton's "Ode on the Morning of Christ's Nativity",' I said modestly.

On the night, the society committee entertained the distinguished guests to a sherry reception in the Common Room before the meeting. The Dining Hall was full as the members of the platform party, in full evening dress and academicals, took their places.

I was nervous as I stood forward to the lectern to read my paper. I was critical of what I saw as the church's problem with the communication of the gospel to a modern world that was crying out for 'good news'. The church was hamstrung by tradition, engrossed in its own importance, absorbed with its own administration and the survival of the institution, all to the detriment of the communication of its central message. As I got going I gained in confidence as I had prepared the paper carefully.

Kennelly talked about communication from the point of view of literature and in particular poetry. The retired bishop from India used his experience as a missionary to make his point about communication. The Professor from Keele took an academic line and the climax of the evening was the speech of Bishop Pike from California who put on an oratorical performance for more than forty minutes and held the packed house in the palm of his hand.

'If you're selling dog meat you can design the most elaborate and eye-catching label for the tin. You can spend a fortune advertising it, you can spend what you like marketing it and distributing it but it won't sell if the dogs don't like it.' He developed this theme using it as an analogy for the challenge of the gospel.

When Peter Odlum received his invitation to the meeting, unknown to me he asked Alleyn Harris to book a table at a nearby restaurant for me and for a number of my friends for after the meeting. PD came himself and of course footed the bill.

In the early days in Castlewood Avenue, while I was still in the mill I had girlfriends on and off, but none too seriously as I would not allow anything to interfere with my plans. I was not prepared to consider anything in this department until I was ordained. I had first met Jennifer in Castlewood Avenue through a fellow we called the Mannequin. I knew him from Leinster-Stratford Tennis Club where I was a pavilion member in order to give me easy access to the regular dances they held in the pavilion. He arrived one night at the flat with two girls in the car and wanted me to go for a drive. I didn't want to go out so they came in and we had coffee in the kitchen where I sat talking to Jennifer while the Mannequin went into the sitting-room with her friend. Jennifer told me she was a Presbyterian from Donegal studying to be a PE teacher at Ling, so I suggested that she should join Adelaide Road Presbyterian Church since there was a good youth club there. She had been reluctant to come in and she was nervous, as her mother had told her when she was coming to Dublin never to go into a man's flat on her own. She sat on the edge of her chair with her hands on the seat, ready to run if anything I said or did looked ominous. She was in no danger whatever. On the contrary, I was protective towards her. Jennifer was at the next Leinster-Stratford dance and she recounted to me later that she thought that at least I would dance with her, but apparently I simply said 'hello' and walked past.

After my first meeting with Jennifer we went out together from time to time. We would go back to the flat for coffee and I would bring her home to her digs in Sandymount on the bar of the bike. She came from an extremely clean and ordered home and found the dirt and disorder of our all male flat hard to take. Forty years later she still talks about the unmade beds and the filthy pillowcases! For me the flat was my home. For the others it was a flat in Dublin. I never felt badly about this, it was just the way it was. I was never short of invitations down the country at weekends or at holidays with my flatmates, and in due course to Jennifer's home in Donegal.

CHAPTER NINE

The States

When I came to live in Dublin first, Patti O'Neill, Iris's younger sister, wrote to me regularly from Moyaliffe and kept me up to date with the news. All these people had been for years as close as I had had to family. I was interested to hear of all the goings-on, for I didn't want to loose touch with them or with the Hanafins. From time to time I went down to Thurles to stay with Des and his family. I looked forward to these weekend visits. If I knew from Patti that Mrs Kemmis and the Captain were away Des would lend me his Volkswagen beetle, which was brave of him, to go out to Moyaliffe to call on the O'Neills in the yard and to the others, and to see the horses and the dogs.

On one of these visits, I went out to the paddock. I called out to Redeye, the old retired horse I used to ride bare-backed around the estate and that I sometimes used for my work with the poultry farm. He lifted his head and looked, and as I called him again, he whinnied and came galloping over. He nuzzled me and I petted him, and I have no doubt he remembered me. When I visited I always saw Silvo, my trusted friend and rat catcher, and later on I was terribly sad to hear from Patti that he was dead. The following day I had a letter from Mrs Kemmis to tell me the same news. Silvo was a young dog the first time I went to Moyaliffe and over the years we had good times together. I missed him on my next visit.

I loved these visits back to Moyaliffe as the place had meant so much to me. I felt, however, I had made the break with Captain and Mrs Kemmis. I was grateful for what they had done for me, but I had moved on and I was doing well in Dublin, so rightly or wrongly I didn't want to complicate my life by becoming in-volved with them again.

I left Moyaliffe in 1951 and it was ten years before I saw the Kemmises again. It was in the late summer just before I entered Trinity. I was walking past Sir Patrick Dun's Hospital and met them coming towards me. The Captain was wearing his jodhpurs and springing up on his toes in his own distinctive way. Mrs Kemmis was her usual charming self, asking the right questions and evaluating everything. They were genuinely glad to see me and I to see them, but I felt I was meeting them on my own ground. Now that I was about to go to Trinity, I have no doubt, I was a notch or two up in their estimation and they asked me if I would go down to Ballinacor to see them. The very day I started in Trinity a letter arrived from the Captain wishing me success in college and containing a £5 note and an invitation to lunch. Though my life had moved on I was glad to re-establish contact with them for they had provided the stable context for so many years of my early life. I accepted their invitation to lunch and for a few hours I returned to that old-fashioned rural gentility that I had almost forgotten existed. It was a world in marked contrast to the world I had lived in for the previous ten years – life in a flat in Rathmines and work in a mill on Dublin's quays. Glad as I was to re-establish contact with Captain and Mrs Kemmis, I was on the road I wanted to travel and I had no desire to be part of their world again.

At the beginning of my third year in college a letter arrived from Mrs Kemmis to say the Captain was ill in St Michael's Hospital Dún Laoghaire. I went out to the hospital regularly to see him and she was always there. She was extremely attentive and did all she could to stop builders in the grounds using pneumatic drills as he found the noise hard to bear. Mrs Kemmis was most appreciative of the surgeon, Mr Peter Ashe, a grandson of Thomas Ashe. In her diaries she recounts what a fine person he was, kind and considerate. Some years later when I broke my leg he attended to me and I can confirm Mrs Kemmis's opinion of him. He was the epitome of kindness and consideration for his patients.

It soon became clear that the Captain was not going to make

it, and on 5 January 1962 he died. When I received the news I
went out to the hospital and Mrs Kemmis was there with Mrs
Lomer, a cousin of the Captain's and mother of Richard who
was to inherit Ballinacor. Mrs Kemmis told me she was expecting Robert Barton from Glendalough and what a wonderful
man he was and he would make arrangements for the funeral.
This was Robert Barton who had been a signatory of the Anglo
Irish Treaty in 1922. There was no sign of him and the hospital
was impatient to have the room. Mrs Kemmis was under pressure when she received a message to confirm he was on his way.
She asked me to go downstairs to meet him. Eventually he arrived, a tall imposing man. I approached him and said 'Mr
Barton.' 'Yes,' he said, 'and who are you?' 'I'm a friend of the
Kemmises.' 'Oh,' he said, 'how good a friend are you?'

I ignored his question. He obviously didn't know the
Captain was dead. I imagine he had come to town and had a
good lunch in the Kildare Street Club and ambled out to see his
old pal. Mrs Kemmis's confidence that he would look after the
funeral was misplaced. At the heel of the hunt I had to arrange
everything including a lead lined coffin because the Captain
was to be placed in the family vault.

We left the hospital at six o'clock on a wet January evening. I
drove Mrs Kemmis and Mrs Lomer in my powder blue Morris
1000 following the hearse along Dún Laoghaire front. We turned
up through Glenageary, left onto Rochestown Avenue and
down into the Captain's beloved Wicklow, through Roundwood,
Laragh and Clara Vale into the village of Greenane, turning right
to the long avenue of Ballinacor.

When the house came into view all the lights were on to welcome the master home for the last time. When they carried the
Captain into the house the men who worked on the estate,
dressed in Sunday best, stood along one side of the wide hall,
some of them with cap in hand. The women servants, in black
with starched white cap and apron, stood down the other side.
The local rector, Jim Farrar, led the cortege into the billiard room
for a short service of reception. It was like a scene from a film. I

had to go with Jennifer to Donegal to her family two days later and I wasn't at the funeral itself which the Archbishop of the Diocese, George Simms, conducted. 'Kemmo' as Mrs Kemmis called him had been a loyal member of his church and parish, and had served on his local select vestry and diocesan council. Members of the local Catholic parish asked to be allowed to escort the coffin down the avenue to Greenane village on its way to Ballinatone Church where the good Captain was laid to rest in his family vault. Local Catholics thought well of him for he was generous in the use he gave them of the estate for their outdoor functions.

Over the next months and years I came to know Mrs Kemmis adult to adult, which was somewhat of an adjustment for her. She was bereft after the Captain died and I undertook in my own mind to look after her. This was often to my own detriment as she was a determined manipulative woman who always put her own interests first. She continued to live at Ballinacor and spent most of her time preparing things for Richard Lomer to take over. I went down often to help her with practicalities. Lomer became impatient to take possession and eight months or so after the Captain's death he put pressure on her to leave. She did not want to go until she could leave everything in pristine order down to the last detail. She even counted items in the linen cupboard to be sure every last napkin was present and correct. Eventually she left with nothing but her own personal belongings. That was the way she wanted it. It was a Kemmis house and according to her value-system nothing belonged to her, an Armstrong.

Some years before, as she and the Captain were getting older and had two estates to run, Mrs Kemmis had made Moyaliffe over to cousins. This didn't work out, mainly, I suspect, because she continued to interfere. They eventually left and the Land Commission decided to take it over, but Mrs Kemmis appealed the decision and won on condition that Moyaliffe could not be sold for three years. She then settled it on a niece from England. This settlement gave her an annuity that diminished significantly with inflation in the seventies. The niece was divorced and re-married and Mrs Kemmis worried how this might affect her standing locally. She and her husband were not happy in Moyaliffe anyway, and as soon as the three years were up they sold the whole place to the Land Commission except for the con-tents of the house, which still belonged to Mrs Kemmis.

As part of the Ballinacor settlement Lomer bought Moyaliffe and 12 acres of curtilage back from the Land Commission for Mrs Kemmis. Since Moyaliffe wasn't available for her to live in when she left Ballinacor, a friend of the Captain, a Colonel Darley gave her the loan of a shooting lodge in Lacken, Co Wicklow. I helped her to move and I supported her as best I could during this difficult time when she was indeed grief-stricken. She believed in God and very much wanted to believe in miracles, mostly to her own benefit. Her God was fashioned much in her own image – a common human failing. The day eventually came for her to return to Moyaliffe. I drove her from Lacken and we arrived at Moyaliffe at about six o'clock. It was a dark wet spring evening. The house was cold. There was no water, light or heat. I got water from the pump in the yard, lit candles and a fire in the smoking room, and cooked her a fry, staple diet of the flat, on a little gas burner I had brought with me, and I helped her to settle in.

The next day a friend of mine brought the rest of her things from Lacken. It was a difficult time for her. The house was damp and neglected but she was a good organiser and in no time she had Moyaliffe back in order again. She arranged for Kate, the cook, and Nora, the housekeeper, to come back. She went to the factory in Thurles where one of the men, Tommy Hayes, now worked. She had him called out from his work and told him it was his duty to come back to Moyaliffe and help to look after it, and he did. I have no doubt he earned a lower wage, but he would have been happier working around Moyaliffe than in the factory in Thurles.

He reclaimed the lawn and declared war on the thistles. He cleared part of the walled garden and grew vegetables for the

house. He was handyman and general factotum and Moyaliffe
was as much part of Tommy as it was of Mrs Kemmis. His father,
Tom, and his grandfather had worked all their lives on the estate. One of Tommy's jobs was to drive Mrs Kemmis in her little
Fiat motor car. She had never driven until the Captain died and
then learned, but never took her test. The truth of the matter was
that both of them knew that Mrs Kemmis could not survive in
Moyaliffe without Tommy, and she would not have been able to
find anybody else to do the work he did.

All this time I was in Trinity and getting on with my studies,
insofar as I ever got on with them. I never got good marks, as I
never applied myself fully to my academic work, but I made
sure to do enough to get through exams. It was all for me a
means to an end – ordination – which by now was looming ever
closer. Mid-way through my final year all my fellow final year
students had completed arrangements for their parish place-
ments. I alone in the year had not yet been appointed to a curacy.
John Brown, the Warden of the Hostel, whose responsibility it
was to arrange interviews for prospective deacons, asked me to
go and see the rector of Clontarf, Canon McCollum. I went out to
see him and we had a good conversation and he showed me
around the parish.

I liked him but deep down I knew it just wasn't the place for
me. Back at the Hostel John Brown sent for me. If you burned
John Brown for a fool you'd have wise ashes.

'Well,' he asked. 'What did you think of Clontarf?'

'What do you think of it?' I asked.

'I didn't bring you here to tell you what I think. I want to
know what you think'

I stuck to my guns.

'I'm not going to tell you my impressions until you tell me
what you think.'

This went on backwards and forwards between us for a few
minutes and then I said:

'Look here John, I give you my word of honour, if you tell me
what you think I will tell you exactly what I think and it won't
be influenced in any way by what you say.'

He gave up the struggle.

'Well Kevin, you know you have a way with you and other people see that, and if you go out to Clontarf I think you would find it far too easy to work with McCollum.' What he meant was that McCollum was too easygoing and would let me do what I liked and that would not be good for me. He would not discipline or train me as a first rector should.

'That is exactly the conclusion I came to myself,' I said. Our views coincided exactly, so I discounted Clontarf with the Warden's approval.

This was March and there didn't seem to be any other openings for me to stay in Dublin, which was what I wanted. I was becoming anxious, for a curacy in the North was staring me in the face, when I remembered what Bishop Pike of California had said, 'You should really come to America and I will help you any way I can.'

Within days of my interview in Clontarf I sent off an application to the World Council of Churches in Geneva to spend a year of study in the United States, stating a preference for Berkeley in California. I waited with trepidation trying to work out what I would do if I didn't get the scholarship and my only option would be a curacy in the North. A month or so later I got a letter to say that I had been awarded a scholarship at the Church Divinity School of the Pacific in Berkeley. I couldn't believe it, and neither could others. The look of total disbelief on the faces of some of my professors and lecturers, including John Brown, had to be seen to be believed. I didn't care what they thought. I was over the moon. There were others like Dr Ernie Nicholson and Tom Salmon who were absolutely delighted for me. When I eventually got to New York and called to the World Council of Churches office I met a Mr Ching, the man responsible for awarding scholarships. 'So you're Kevin Dalton. Well I want to tell you something, Mr Dalton, when I read your cv I said to myself: "This guy just has to get what he wants".'

In the meantime I was something of a loose canon – a year in the States in prospect and no parish to come home to, but my final exams were looming and that kept me from thinking about it until one afternoon in the Hostel John Brown sent for me. There was a clergyman I didn't know with him. It was Marcus Taylor, rector of Stillorgan, who was looking for a curate. John Brown introduced us and left us together. We talked for a while and Marcus told me about his parish and what he would expect from a curate, but without committing himself. He and John Brown came outside with me and I left them to drive down town and kicked up some gravel as I took off. John told me later that Marcus turned to him and said, 'If he drives like that he'll do me.' In due course Marcus wrote to me offering the curacy and stating the stipend – £600 per year. The plan was that I would be ordained deacon in June and in August go to California for a year and be ordained priest when I returned to Stillorgan parish the following July.

There was a story to this appointment. Some weeks previously Marcus Taylor had taken the funeral of Colonel Hume Dudgeon, the famous horseman of Burton Hall. After the burial a man he didn't know came over to him in the churchyard and said:

'I want to give you £7,000 for the parish for some useful purpose in memory of Hume Dudgeon, he was a great friend of mine.'

'You're not serious,' said Marcus.

'Of course I'm bloody well serious,' said the stranger.

For some time before this Marcus had been trying to get together the money to finance a curate, but without success. Then this offer was made. He invested the money and on the strength of it he planned to buy a curate's house and then went to see John Brown. I was available, we liked each other and Marcus appointed me with the agreement that I take up my scholarship first. Again a door had been opened unexpectedly.

John Galvin was the wealthy benefactor who, by coincidence, also knew Mrs Kemmis. Shortly after she heard of these developments she invited him for lunch and put it to him that while I was in the States I would need a car. She knew he was a

man of substance and it wasn't in her nature to let a man of substance off scot-free. In fact he was a Roman Catholic and a Papal
Knight and had been involved with many charities in Ireland including the new St Vincent's Hospital on Merrion Road.

After his visit to Mrs Kemmis John Galvin invited me to his
home, Loughlinstown House, one evening for dinner. It was a
barbeque on the lawn and I was sitting beside him. He chatted in
a friendly way to me about Mrs Kemmis, my appointment to
Stillorgan and my impending year in California.

'How will you be for money when you get to the States?'

Here I was sitting in the garden of this mansion talking to a
man I had never met before in my life, and though I was never
full of pride I had a certain amount of self-respect.

'Oh, I'll manage,' I said, with a hefty overdraft in the bank
after five years in college. He didn't say anything further of the
matter until he was helping me on with my coat as I was about
to leave.

'Mr Dalton, what I really meant to say was have you money
to buy yourself a car when you get to America?'

I looked him straight in the eye and said:

'No, I have not.'

'Well,' he said. 'Will you go and see my attorney in San
Francisco when you get to California?'

'Yes, I will.'

'Good, I'll meet you at the rectory in the morning and bring
you the papers.'

True to his word next day he brought me a letter of introduc-
tion to his attorney in San Francisco.

My final exams were ahead and I passed them in the same
way I passed all my other exams in College – just about. Next
was ordination. First of all there were the practicalities – fees for
examinations, legal fees, money to buy a suit and robes, but after
five years as a student I was broke. In fact with the help of the
bank I was more than broke. There was an ordination grant from
the Church Body but given the parlous state of my finances it
was no more than a drop in the ocean. I wrote with little convic-

tion and a great deal of hope to the Church Grants Committee and asked them to clear my overdraft of £350, a sizeable sum in those days. I was greatly surprised and equally pleased some weeks later to receive from the Committee a cheque for that amount.

This meant I was not in debt to the bank, but I had immediate expenses to meet in preparation for ordination. I approached three people who had supported me so generously in every way during my life to date and each of whom I knew would be glad that I asked: Miss Carr, Mrs Kemmis and P. D. Odlum. Miss Carr paid my examination fees, Mrs Kemmis my graduation expenses and PD bought my degree hood. I particularly wanted each of these three who had done so much for me over the years to be associated with this important occasion in my life. Each of them contributed willingly and PD seemed to be particularly pleased to have been asked.

I was ordained with a friend Don McClatchie, and George Simms, the Archbishop who ordained us, conducted our ordination retreat himself. I was not a great subject for a retreat but I remember his theme: *'O Sacerdos quid es? Nihil et omnia.'* 'O priest, what are you? Nothing and everything.' The ordination took place on 16 June 1966, the Third Sunday after Trinity in the Church of St John the Baptist, Clontarf, where Don had been appointed curate by Canon McCollum. Dean Salmon preached on the call of the disciples by Jesus as he walked by the Sea of Gallilee. He was a good preacher, and as he had been so supportive of me I was glad he was there. The church was virtually full and there were people there from various stages of my life. Mrs Kemmis came and I could not help remembering her reply to me when I was eleven or twelve when she asked me what I wanted to be when I grew up and I had without hesitation replied: 'A clergyman,' and her reply: 'Oh, that could never be.'

Miss Carr was there and P. D. Odlum, and of course Jennifer. There were friends from college, the Harding, the flat, the now defunct poker school and the mill. Dermot Mooney, a shop steward at the mill, told me he rang the Roman Catholic

Archbishop's house to know if he could go to my ordination.
They asked him a lot of questions on the phone such as was I related or how did he know me and for how long, and then the
priest to whom he spoke said:

'Write it all down and send it in and we will consider the
matter.'

'I will not,' he said, 'Good day,' and he turned up at the ordination. Des Hanafin was there, in good order. These were still
his drinking days. After the service he wanted particularly to
meet Archbishop Simms who received him graciously. Despite
his problem drinking Des had a strong spiritual sense, which
eventually helped him to overcome his addiction.

Some weeks beforehand I was talking to Mrs Kemmis about
the ordination. She asked me about the day itself and I told her
about the service and that I would have to have some kind of reception afterwards. She knew I had less than no money.

'You'll have to pay for that,' I said, and to be fair to her, without flinching, she agreed. In all the years I had known her, apart
from my graduation expenses and this, I don't believe I had ever
before asked her for anything. I told myself that it was only fair
that she should compensate me for her lack of confidence that I
would achieve my ambition! So after the service I retired with
my friends to the Old Sheeling Hotel in Raheny for tea.

My ordination meant a huge amount to me. The service and
the day were the realisation of a dream I had had since I was a
young boy. It was a dream, a call, a persistent hound that would
not let go. It was always there, in the background or in the fore-
ground. Sometimes it was stronger than other times. When we
were young together Des Hanafin was going to be a TD and I
was going to be a clergyman and that was why it was so important to me that he was present at my ordination. When Des con-
quered his problem, in due course he became a senator.

Despite having worked so hard for it, I looked on my ordination as an expected happening that I had anticipated for a long
time. The anticipation of it became part of who I was. It was the
fulfilment of my life's ambition to date. I never wanted anything

more than to be a parish clergyman, and while I was happy to achieve it, when it came I took it in my stride. I was never in any doubt about the purpose of my life and once I started on the road there was always help along the way.

The evening of my ordination I preached at Evening Prayer in Stillorgan and took up my duties as curate in the parish until I was due to go to America. At the beginning of July Marcus went on holiday and I was in charge of the parish on my own for a month. What I remember most of this period was having three services by myself every Sunday: Family Service at 10.00 am, Morning Prayer or Communion at 11.15 am and Evening Prayer at 7.00 pm, and having to preach a different sermon at each service. Apart from leaving me with three sermons a Sunday while he was away, Marcus was good to me, supporting and guiding me in the work.

The parish planned to buy a curate's house when I came back from the States so until I was due to go I lodged with a Mrs Bradford. Charlie, as she was known, could not have been kinder to her bachelor guest. Her maid, Kate, ran the bath and left out towels for me, and if Charlie thought I needed shirts or socks she went off and bought them without a word. One evening Jennifer phoned while I was working on a sermon. 'Tell her I'm busy,' I said, 'I'll phone her back.' Well she nearly put me out of the house. 'Go and speak to her immediately,' and I did. When I was getting ready to leave for America she saw my dilapidated cardboard suitcase and went out and bought me a proper one. I had never been so well looked after in my life; nobody had ever cosseted me in this way before.

One day a few weeks before my ordination I was down at the mill. Peter Odlum, who had heard about my year in America, cross-examined me about it in great detail. Then he said, 'When you go to America it won't be the same as driving around the south of Ireland in your Morris Minor with your sleeping bag in the boot. You'll need money, and I want you to write and tell me what you need.' Then he looked me straight in the eye and said sternly: 'And Kevin, if you don't let me know we will not be friends.' And just before I left he said, 'Kevin, don't forget if you don't tell me what you need we won't be friends.'

Shortly before I was due to leave I wrote to him and told him I needed £300. He sent me a cheque by return of post with a warm letter wishing me well. Six or seven years before when I told him I was planning to go to Trinity to train for ordination he had said, 'I'll help you any way I can,' and he had been every bit as good as his word.

The day before I was due to sail for America a friend drove me down to Moyaliffe and we stayed the night with Mrs Kemmis. Next morning he drove me to Galway where I went out on a tender to board the *Maas Dan* for the voyage across the Atlantic. I enjoyed the voyage but many of the passangers were seasick. I was all right because I ate sparingly or not at all. Two Texans, a father and son, couldn't resist the temptation to eat their fill at every meal and soon afterwards they would head for the side of the ship and project the lot into the ocean.

I found it evocative to sail into New York harbour and past Ellis Island and the Statue of Liberty, for it reminded me of the millions of poor Irish emigrants of previous generations who had had to leave Ireland for America in order to survive, and the many that didn't survive the voyage or got no further than Ellis Island. I have always had a soft spot for the United States for this reason: it provided a home and the opportunity of human dignity to so many of my fellow countrymen and women.

In New York I met with other WCC scholarship students from around the world for an orientation course. Mr Ching, who had viewed my application for a scholarship so favourably, conducted the course that gave us a flavour of what to expect during our stay in America. It had been arranged that during the course I would stay with a couple in Larchmount, outside the city. Ann was born in America of a Church of Ireland family from County Down and had responded to an announcement in her local parish church asking for accommodation for a deacon from Dublin. As an Anglican deacon from the South of Ireland I was somewhat of an oddity. I was not used to the oppressive heat and that day I had three showers to try to keep cool, and the fact that I was wearing a black suit with a stock and dog collar didn't help. It took Jennifer six years to get me out of such traditional dress. Ann's husband, Pete, welcomed me warmly but I thought I detected some slight unease. He walked in and out of the kitchen a number of times and eventually uttered the magic words, 'Would you like a drink?' 'What have you got?' I asked, and the whole atmosphere changed. He named a string of drinks, most of which I had never heard of. I recognised the name 'Scotch' and I settled for that. It was the first time, but not the last, that I drank whiskey. From then on Pete and I got on famously.

On my second night there Ann lent me her car and I drove into New York, to Lexington Avenue to see Chris Keag, an old friend who had worked in the mill. He and his wife Kathleen, who was from Kerry, took me out for a drink to a singing pub where late in the evening a black man stood up on a table and sang 'America, America'. It was a great night and in the small hours of the morning I drove back to Larchmount where Pete and Ann were relieved to find the car and me all in one piece.

Before I left New York I made my way to Arlington Cemetery near Washington, to visit the grave of John F. Kennedy. During the days after his assassination I had promised myself that if I ever got to America I would do just that. Whatever the faults of his personal life, he had paid Ireland a huge compliment by visiting us for three days. When he was in Dublin a friend and I crashed a reception in Dublin Castle in the guise of 'Press' to see him receiving the freedom of the city. The impact he made on so many was a welcome breath of fresh air, full of hope and promise.

After New York I had time to travel before I was due in Berkeley. Before leaving Dublin I had bought for $99 a 99-day Greyhound bus ticket, available only outside the United States, by which I could travel as far as I liked on the Greyhound bus network within 99 days of the first journey. I decided to get value for my money. I was determined to see as much as possible of this country I knew so well from the Penguin *A History of the United States* in two volumes, and from regular reading of *Time* magazine.

I persuaded Mr Ching to make arrangements for me to stay on my travels in Episcopal seminaries free of charge. My first trip was upstate New York to see June O'Connor, the girl I had been found with in the wardrobe in Miss Carr's Home, as a result of which incident I was quickly despatched to the Havergal twenty five years before. This time it was purely a social call. I discovered she was married with two children. She and her husband gave me a warm welcome and took me off for a day to Niagara Falls. June and I talked a bit about our time in the home (no mention was made of the incident in the wardrobe!) and about what had happened to each of us since. She and her husband were a conservative couple with whom I had little in common, but I enjoyed seeing her again.

I left Rochester and made my way to Richmond, Virginia to see Jimmy Dwyer who had worked on Moyaliffe and whose American wake I had been at before he left for the States. Both he and Alice, his wife, gave me a terrific welcome. Jimmy worked in a hospital laboratory nearby but he took time off to show me around In particular he brought me to the restored town of Williamsburgh, of War of Independence fame. Jimmy had done well, and though nostalgic about Ireland and glad to hear news of some of the people he had worked with at Moyaliffe, he was proud of his adopted country.

One of the girls I met on the ship on the way over had given me the address of an Irish Catholic priest, Noel Buttenshaw, in Atlanta. He was Chancellor of the Archdiocese. I phoned him and he gave me a warm welcome. I had an interesting couple of days with him before going on to New Orleans, where I stayed at the Episcopal seminary and spent an evening at Preservation Hall.

From New Orleans I took the bus to Austin, Texas, again to stay at the Episcopal seminary there. It arrived late on Saturday evening and on Sunday morning I went to the early eucharist in the college chapel. It was out of term time but there were about

thirty people present and I went around to the sacristy to intro-
duce myself and say 'hello'. I explained who I was and why I
was there. The man counting the collection said, 'You're the
very person. You've been sent to us. You can tell us all about the
Church of Ireland.' So there and then I had to stand up and talk
to the whole group about the church and Christianity in Ireland.
Those present were a group of local people who had left their
parish with the blessing of their rector and bishop. They were a
kind of official church house-group who met every Sunday
morning for Communion at the seminary.

They were evangelical and they were feeling their way in a
new situation. I told them about the Church of Ireland in the
Republic, something of its history and what it was like to be a
member of a small minority Anglican Church in a predominantly
conservative Roman Catholic country. I talked for about half an
hour and then had questions and discussion. They were interested
and grateful for my talk that had given them something to think
about. They insisted on giving me an honorarium which I tried,
unsuccessfully, to refuse! After the talk one of the group drove
me to Dallas to meet their mentor, a well-known writer and
evangelist, Keith Miller.

After Dallas I went to San Antonio and went to see the big
naval base there, but by this time I was impatient to get to
Berkeley. I had read about Telegraph Avenue and the Flower
People and all the exciting things that happened there. Of course
I was impatient too to see the Church Divinity School of the
Pacific and meet the people with whom I would spend the next
year. The following morning I got on the bus for the long journey to Berkeley, found CDSP and reported to the Dean,
Sherman Johnston. He was the man who had turned the school
into a significant seminary in the Episcopal Church and had
started the graduate course I was now joining. He welcomed me
and arranged for someone to bring me to my room, which
would be my accommodation for the academic year, and to
show me around the college.

The next day I crossed Bay Bridge to San Francisco to see

John Galvin's attorney. The first thing he said to me was, 'If you don't mind my saying so, you should be wearing a tie. You don't come into the city in an open-necked shirt.' I did mind, and in other circumstances I'd have taken him on, but I swallowed it because as far as the car was concerned he held all the cards. I didn't like the guy, but after some paper work he brought me to a garage and bought me a three-year-old yellow Galaxy 500 which wasn't top of the range but it certainly wasn't bottom either. He taxed and insured it and gave me $750 for gas. I drove that car all over California and because of John Galvin's generosity I ended up knowing that part of America better than many of my fellow students who came from there.

Before Christmas I wrote to John Galvin and gave him an account of my time in California. I thanked him for the car that had given me such freedom and independence. He was particularly interested in the work of the Spanish priest Father Junipero Serra who had founded the nine California Missions. They stretch from San Diego in the south to Sanoma in the north with a distance of a day's journey by mule separating them. During my time in California I visited all of them and took slides that I brought home to him as a 'thank you' for his generosity.

The school itself was a stimulating place to be. It was on a different scale from the Divinity School in Trinity, where there were three fulltime and five or six parttime lecturers to 60 students. CDSP had ten fulltime and eight parttime lecturers for about one hundred students. Among the faculty were some well-known scholars: Sherman Johnston a New Testament scholar, Massey Sheppard a world-class liturgist, who was a member of a Commission of the Archbishop of Canterbury to Rome, Samuel Garrett, a noted historian, who had a great love for the Church of Ireland, and another faculty member was a noted scholar who was part of the then current theological fashion, the 'God is Dead' movement.

The argument was that the concept 'God' was meaningless in modern society, and that to all intents and purposes God was dead for twentieth century man. This debate nearly floored me.

Having worked so hard to get there I didn't want my God to be dead so soon after being ordained. During my first term I had to write an essay on the subject and ended it with the quotation attributed to Mary in St John's Gospel: 'They have taken away my Lord and I know not where they have laid him.' My tutor for this essay was an Australian who had not bought into the movement and approved of my essay. I found this reassuring. A few years later, as with many fashions from America, the 'God is Dead' movement itself died as some other fashion attracted.

It took me a while to settle down at CDSP. I was homesick – a strange thing for one who didn't actually have a home. I missed Jennifer, I missed Ireland and I missed familiar people and places. The never changing blue sky made me long to see a cloud. I couldn't even get a decent cup of tea; there were tea bags, which I had never seen before, and luke warm water. For a while I resorted to drinking coffee. It's missing the people that make you homesick and the little things rub it in.

The most significant friendship I made during my time in Berkeley was with Colby and Ann Cogswell. Colby, who was chaplain to the Divinity School, had been a vice-president of Wells Fargo Bank, that romantic name from cowboy films. Wells Fargo is a major bank in the United States, and Colby still did some parttime work for them. When he was appointed chaplain he and his family had moved up from Palo Alto to Brookside in Berkeley. He and his wife Ann were two of nature's lovely people. He realised early on that I hadn't settled, that I was homesick. One day I was with Colby and Ann, when Colby took me upstairs and showed me a self-contained suite, 'Kevin, I'm going to give you a key to here and you can come down any time you like; you can use it as long as you are here.' I did use it and I met Colby and Ann's daughter Ryrie and their 14-year-old son Will. In the move to Berkeley Will had been uprooted from his friends and was missing them terribly, so we had much in common and we got on like a house on fire. He was 14 and I was 34 going on 14. We were somehow perfectly matched and we fought like cats over board-games and what TV channel to watch. I kept contact with the Cogswells over the years and 20 years after I returned to Ireland I had a letter from Will saying how important that part of his life had been. Colby and Ann treated me as part of the family, which included a dachshund called Freddie, the most obedient dog I ever met, and a cat called Wilbur.

Fellow students invited me to their homes, one of whom was Chuck Stacey. His father was rector of a parish in King City and I went there for a weekend. Another, Larry Hall, is now rector of one of the largest churches in America, St John the Evangelist, Houston. There was a Chinese guy who later became Bishop of Antarctica; does anyone live in the Antarctic? Anyway he became bishop of somewhere like that. John Hinds was son of the Presiding Bishop of the Episcopal Church. There was another WCC scholarship student there from England, with whom I never hit it off. In the beginning I was in bad form anyway and I rubbed him up the wrong way about the Brits' record in Ireland and it inevitably made things worse.

With the freedom the car gave me I travelled around California. Most weekends I went somewhere – to Yosemite National Park, to Fort Brag in northern California among the redwoods to preach in a country church. I also had some addresses from friends in Ireland of people to look up. A parishioner in St Ann's gave me the address in San Francisco of a woman, Merveen Wilson, a friend of his wife, who was originally from Belfast. One evening early on I called to see her. A particularly good-looking young woman, wearing nothing but a bath towel answered the door. 'Have I come all the way from Ireland to see a vision like this?' I said. Merveen wasn't there so Jennifer in the bath towel invited me in to wait for her. Jennifer was going out on a date and left me in the house on my own. As she left I said, 'Don't be late home.' She was back in about an hour and she, Merveen, Cynthia, who lived there too, and I had a great evening together. Jennifer was en route to Vancouver and left in a few weeks. Merveen and Cynthia became friends of mine and anytime I was at a loose end I would go and spend time with them. They included me in their own social events and they were careful to tell me of anything of interest happening on the Irish scene in San Francisco.

As part of my course I was placed for practical work in an Anglican parish, El Sobrante, north of Berkeley, where the rector was a Father Ed Perrott. He asked me to help in the parish youth club, which I did. After Christmas I went with the youth club on a skiing trip to Lake Tahoe where I quickly discovered that skiing was yet another sport I could make no impression upon. Around this time Helene Snell arrived from England to work as a nurse at the local hospital in El Sobrante. Her landlady, a Mrs Blount, introduced her to the parish.

Mrs Blount was a widow whose life revolved around going to church and having parties. She was a good woman and she was kind to Helene, who had been followed out to California by a man from England who was determined to marry her. Helene had serious reservations about this man, but Mrs Blount was all for it, and had already put in place plans for a large party after the wedding. Although the date was set Helene had confided in me that she was not at all certain about marrying this fellow. Three days before the wedding I called to the hospital and told her to tell the fellow to go home, she was about to make a terrible mistake. She did. She knew it was the right thing to do, but she wanted somebody else to tell her. It wasn't the most sophisticated piece of counselling on my part, but I knew she didn't want to marry the guy. Mrs Blount was terribly disappointed – she had to cancel her party. Six months later Helene met Michael, whom she married in due course and she's still happily married to him. When I go to California I always go to see them.

My first term between September and Christmas was tough. Despite all the kindness and hospitality and although I attended lectures I couldn't settle down to study. Jennifer wrote to me weekly and I wrote back, but according to her not often enough. I wrote also to friends and tried to exorcise my homesickness by describing life in California. I wrote a long letter to Peter Odlum and described the huge highways and intersections and how they were eating up the fertile land and destroying the land-scape. I was critical of California and its way of life, the rootless-ness of the people and their lack of community and belonging. He was delighted to get the letter and replied saying how much he enjoyed reading it. I felt that because I was unhappy I was hypercritical and more perceptive about the society I was living in.

Towards the end of the first term I made up my mind that, however I managed it, I would go home for Christmas. Jennifer was delighted. She thought I should have brought her with me to California in the first place, but that would have been imprac-tical – what would we have lived on? My $99 dollar bus ticket was still valid so it took me three days non-stop travelling by bus to get to New York. I arrived exhausted to get a flight to Shannon. I spent a few days in Dublin seeing friends and then went to Donegal to spend Christmas with Jennifer and her family.

While I was home I met Dermot Molloy from the mill who told me Peter Odlum was expecting me to call. I hadn't planned to see him as I was short of time, but I went immediately and he was delighted. Again he told me not to hesitate to contact him if I was short of money and he reached into a drawer and took out a cheque for £50. 'I heard you were coming home and I've had this waiting for you,' he said.

After Christmas when I arrived at Shannon to fly back to America the flight was delayed. It was delayed four times and I made up my mind that if it didn't take off after the fourth delay I wasn't going to board that plane. I didn't believe it would make it to New York. I even phoned a friend in Limerick for a bed for the night, but the flight did in fact go and I arrived back safely in California. It was a wise decision to go home for Christmas. It worked wonders and when I got back to California I had no problem settling down to work, and I was much happier.

CDSP had told me they would give me credit for two years of their three-year BD degree in lieu of theology I had done in Trinity. They would award the degree after my year's work if I passed the exams in June. So here I was, a person without any academic distinction or pretension, with the possibility of arriving back in Ireland sporting a BD. There was, however, a snag. They told me that my work at the end of the first term was not up to scratch and warned me that if it didn't improve they wouldn't allow me sit the exam in June. This helped to focus my mind. I couldn't ignore this kind of challenge and so in the new term I knuckled down to work. I was happier and more settled and began to enjoy the study and in fact worked harder than I had ever worked in my five years in Trinity.

I did not, however, go overboard altogether – I still took time off to do other things. On St Patrick's Day the Dean asked me to preach in the Divinity School Chapel. Two of my friends, Larry Hall and Chuck Stacey got to work on a 20 foot x 2 foot banner and strung it across the main building: 'St Patrick's Day Service – Preacher – The Rev Kevin Dalton from Ireland.'

That night Merveen, Cynthia and a couple more friends or-ganised a St Patrick's Day party. They showed a Bord Fáilte film and plied the guests with Gaelic coffees.

Shortly after this The Irish Society in San Francisco invited me to talk to a meeting on 'Ireland Today'. I said that recently the Irish people had had a boost to their confidence in their own national identity. This, I suggested, was due to three recent events:

1. The deaths of 16 Irish soldiers on UN duty in the Congo.
2. The fact that President Kennedy had seen fit to spend three days in Ireland.
3. The recent commemoration of the 1916 Rising.

I maintained that these three events, occurring in the space of about six years, had given people a new pride in being Irish. We were maturing as a nation, even though we were still a poor country dominated by the Roman Catholic Church which had a say in virtually everything, including government legislation. Things were changing slowly, however, after Vatican II, with some help from Gay Byrne and his hugely popular Late Late Show.

During the discussion that followed a speaker challenged me with: 'You'd have to admit that Protestants in the Republic have been shown a great deal of tolerance by the nationalist majority.' I replied: 'That may be your view, but I refuse to thank anybody for tolerating me in my own country. I am every bit as Irish as anybody else in Ireland. It's time we moved away from that kind of thinking. Have you forgotten all the great Irish leaders who were Protestant? Not least Wolf Tone, Emmet and Parnell, and you say I should be grateful for being tolerated.' This inter-action went down particularly well with the CDSP faculty mem-bers who were present.

When the exams came in June I had done a fair amount of work. I found it difficult to know the standard required, but I was determined to pass. In addition to the exams the school took continual assessment into account: written work during the year, my work at the youth club at El Sobrante, any public speaking or preaching I did, and my ability to relate to people. At least I knew I had some chance since they allowed me to sit the exams. When the results came out I had passed comfortably. Graduation Day was a big event at the school with bishops and other bigwigs present and a formal dinner in the evening. Most of the friends I had made in California came – Merveen, Cynthia, Helene and a number of other parishioners from El Sobrante. I knew my BD degree would not have been awarded if I had not deserved it. I felt I had done more work in six months in CDSP than in five years in Trinity.

California and CDSP were stimulating places to be in the 1960s. You could almost touch the atmosphere of freedom in the air. There was room for people with all sorts of ideas. People were accepted for who they were. This was refreshing to me from a conservative island church and a conservative country. The free spirit I encountered in Berkeley permeated every aspect of life there. At first I found it difficult to cope with, but I soon came to value what that society on the western seaboard of the United States was saying about the importance for individuals of being free to explore for themselves. Indeed I can remember on more than one occasion standing in the grounds of the school, taking a deep breath and thinking how good it was to be in a free and open society.

John Galvin's car had been a godsend. It made all the difference to my stay in California. The arrangement he had made
was that before I left I was to sell it and keep the proceeds. About
a month before I was due to leave a fellow student offered me
$900 for it. That was a lot of money to one who had very little
and I was tempted. I resisted the temptation, however, as with a
month to go I didn't want my wings clipped. To be stuck in
Berkeley for four weeks without a car was unthinkable. I eventually sold it on the day I left for $700.

I was tempted to travel home via the east and see another
part of the world, but I had promised Marcus I would return as
soon as I had finished in California to allow him to go on holiday. CDSP kindly gave me the price of an air ticket to New York.
This saved me from another three-day bus journey across the
country. There was, however, one more thing I wanted to do before I left North America. To see the Rockies had been a dream
of mine since I was a small boy, so I flew to Portland, Oregon,
took a bus to Vancouver and then a train through the Canadian
Rockies to Calgary. These majestic mountains exceeded my expectation. It had been well worth the detour. I stayed with Sam
Mehaffy, my former flatmate, and his wife in Calgary for a couple of nights and then flew to New York and home.

When I arrived home Jennifer met me at the airport with my
blue Morris 1000. I drove into the city and was astounded that
there were almost no brakes. We had our first row, as I was astounded that she had been driving the car around in that condition. I was shocked at the state of the brakes because they were
in contrast to the brakes of the car I drove in the States which
when applied sharply would stick the car to the road. The row
didn't last long, however, as we were both delighted to be together again and I had the brakes seen to next day.

Within a couple of days I was back to work in the parish and
I stayed at the rectory until we were married in September.
George Simms, the Archbishop, took a great interest in my
American studies – he liked his clergy to do further study.
Having examined me closely on the content of my BD he ex-

empted me from the usual priests' exams and ordained me priest in the parish church. Bishop Hodges preached the sermon. He had confirmed me hurriedly twenty years earlier on the night before I left the Havergal on my way to Dublin before going to Moyaliffe to run the poultry farm. The only thing I remember of what he said was that when he walked down the street in his gaiters youngsters would click their tongues and shout after him, 'Where'd ye leave the horse?'

CHAPTER TEN

Stillorgan

After the ordination Marcus went on holiday. I was in the parish on my own again, and there was an early Communion and three other services in the parish every Sunday. I was still too green to do other than write three different sermons. I did so because there were some 'twicers' who went to two services. Otherwise I was something of a caretaker doing the essentials, conducting the occasional funeral or baptism, and keeping an eye on everything. Despite the bits and pieces of preaching and pastoral work I had done in California I was still a raw recruit. From my time in St Ann's I knew how a parish worked. I had a fair idea of the human dynamics and the politics that went to make for the cut and thrust of parish life.

I spent most of my time visiting. I disliked it intensely, for I never knew what was waiting behind the hall-door. Generally speaking people were kind and encouraging, but one afternoon I knocked on a door and got no answer. As I approached the next house on my list I could see people peeping out at me from behind the curtains. I rang on the doorbell, but they didn't answer the door. I rang again and listened to be sure the bell worked. It did. I waited, but still nobody answered, so I moved on to a third house. I rang the bell and a woman answered the door and before I could say a word she said in a pronounced English accent, 'No, not today, thank you.' And closed the door. I gave up and went home.

I had better luck the next day. In the first house I called to the woman had a litter of wirehaired dachshund puppies. She picked one up and handed it to me. 'There,' she said, 'You can have this fellow as a wedding present.' We called him 'Scruffy' and he was part of the family for fourteen years.

Marcus had always impressed on me that loyalty was a quality he prized in a colleague. One day I visited a house where the woman began to complain to me bitterly about the rector, so I said to her straight out: 'You had better say all that to the rector to his face. I'm only the curate.'

The first item on the agenda, however, when Marcus returned from holiday was Jennifer and my wedding that was planned for Stillorgan parish church. Jennifer and I had been seeing each other, on and off, for six years. We had had our ups and downs, and Jennifer was never short of admirers, some of whom I knew. Occasionally she would become impatient with me and threaten to call it a day and, knowing the others were waiting like snakes in the grass watching their chance, I was always ready to eat humble pie. Marriage was a big commitment for a fella' of 35 who had been as free a free spirit as I had been all his life, and Jenny understood this in a way few others did. Our wedding was planned for September, which didn't leave much time to make arrangements. Not that I made many, Jennifer did most of the work. I did, however, post the invitations. When I was considering who to ask to be my best man Jenny vetoed one particular friend whom she claimed would not get me there on time, if at all. She approved of Paddy, her final choice and made him promise to call to her on the morning of the wedding to confirm that I was still in the country.

I co-operated fully in all the plans, including turning up for the rehearsal in the church the evening before. After the rehearsal the best man, groomsman and ushers took me to a restaurant in Stepaside for something to eat. Now I didn't drink much in those days and every time they bought me a drink it was a double so that at the end of the night I was, to say the least, in good form. That wasn't a problem. The problem was next morning. I had the mother and father of a headache that no aspirin or such would shift. Finally I decided the only cure would be a hair of the dog that bit me, so with my best man we went to

Mooney's in Dún Laoghaire where with less than an hour to go
we were still sitting on high stools discussing the merits and de-
merits of commitment and marriage. Suddenly Paddy looked at
his watch, jumped down and made for the door. I followed and
we drove to Stillorgan rectory, changed into our monkey-suits
and arrived at the church a matter of minutes before the bride.
My best man was in a worse state of anxiety than I was.

George Simms was to have married us but in the end he
wasn't able to, but came later to the reception. Jim Hartin, Sub-
Warden of the Hostel, conducted the service. The reception was
in the Royal Marine Hotel, Dún Laoghaire. The guests included
of course Jennifer's family and friends. On my side there were
friends from different periods of my life most of whom had been
to my ordination a little over a year before: Miss Carr, Mrs
Kemmis and P. D. Odlum. There were friends from the Harding
and the flat, from the mill and from Trinity. There were even
friends from California. We spent our honeymoon touring
around the South and West of Ireland.

There was a high percentage of couples with teenage children in the parish of Stillorgan. Marcus had told me in the first
place that youth work would have to be my priority. In fact he
left the parish in no doubt that the new curate in California
would work wonders with the youth of the parish when he
came back. When I returned from my honeymoon he reminded
me of this. That was it, no directions, no suggestions and typical
of Marcus, no constraints.

I set a date for a first meeting of what I hoped would be the
beginning of a youth club, and I asked myself over and over
again, 'What, in God's name am I going to do with these kids?' I
hadn't any answers, I simply had no idea, in fact I was scared
stiff, especially as Marcus had given the parish such a high expectation. There was nothing in my training to prepare me for
such a challenge. For that was how I saw it, as a challenge. In
desperation I phoned a curate friend in Belfast and asked him
what I should do. He said, 'Get them together, divide them into
groups of four with paper and pencil and get them to write

down what they think a parish youth club should be. Then bring them back together and discuss their ideas. That will get you over the first night.' Eleven youngsters turned up and he was right. It worked, and we used their ideas for the following couple of nights to plan what we would do. The same eleven along with many more were still members of the youth club when I left the parish four years later.

We decided to run a coffee evening and small sale to raise funds. I announced in church that the young people would be calling to every house in the parish to ask for a contribution in cash or in kind for the sale, to be run by the young people themselves. It was a great success. They made £100 (€1,300 approx, in today's money) to get the club going. We ran dances and discos for the teenagers. We ran folk Communions at which the youngsters provided the music. These Communions were at 8.00 am on Sunday mornings. We gave every member a card with the phone number of another member on it, and when each received a phone call early on Sunday morning, they were to ring the number on the card immediately to remind the other. This way every member received a reminder and we normally had a full attendance. I learned afterwards that although the youngsters responded well to their early morning call, some of their parents weren't enamoured with it. After the service, teams of the members took it in turn to provide breakfast for everybody in that part of the parish hall we called the clubhouse.

The Church of Ireland Bishop of Limerick at this time was a man by the name of Wyse Jackson. He was a Swift scholar who was also concerned about the neglected and derelict state of rural churchyards in his diocese. He wrote a letter to the *Church of Ireland Gazette* to ask if some parishioners from urban parishes would be prepared to go down the country to areas that were sparsely populated with Church of Ireland people to help them clean up neglected churchyards. After early Communion on Sunday mornings, when it wasn't a youth service, I used to go back with Marcus to the rectory for breakfast. One Sunday he threw me a copy of the *Church of Ireland Gazette* and pointing out

Wyse Jackson's letter he said, 'There's the very thing for you and the youth club.'

The idea caught my imagination and I put it to the youngsters. They agreed that it would be worth trying, and that was the beginning of their annual summer project for the next four years. At their weekly meeting the young people spent some of their time planning and fund raising, by discos and dances, for their summer project down the country. No matter what way we looked at it it was going to cost money to get 15 or 20 of them all the way to Kerry for a week or ten days and back again. We devised a scheme by which Stillorgan parishioners in their cars drove them as far as Portlaoise and Portlaoise parishioners, organised by the local rector, drove them to Limerick and Limerick parishioners were recruited by the Dean to drive them the rest of the way to Kerry. We put into operation the same plan in reverse on the way back. With three or four to a car there wasn't room for most of their bags so a Stillorgan parishioner, who was managing director of a large company that distributed throughout the country, arranged for one of his vans to collect most of the luggage a day or two before our departure from the parish hall and deliver it in Kerry for us.

These work parties fulfilled a number of valuable functions. They helped to reclaim overgrown churchyards, but they also let city youngsters see life at first hand in the depths of the country. In particular they saw life in sparsely populated Church of Ireland parishes. The local parishioners not only had their churchyards put in order, but they also saw a group of lively Church of Ireland young people that gave them great encouragement for the future of the church where their numbers were small and their own young people were few.

The first year we went to Milltown in Kerry where the rector, Chris Warren, a bachelor, lived on his own in a big old rectory and had all the youngsters to stay in the house. They all had sleeping bags and some were on beds and others on the floor. A different team of four members prepared breakfast and cooked the evening meal each day. Chris was remarkably patient to ac-

commodate such an invasion. We hired a minibus and drove out
to Dingle every day and cleaned up the churchyard and painted
the church. The day before we were due to leave we finished the
job in the afternoon and, while some of the kids were collecting
up the tools, two others came to me and asked, 'Are we not
going to have a service in the church before we go?' That was
something that I should have been suggesting but I never
thought of it. 'Sure,' I said and before our final barbeque that
night we had a service to which some of the parishioners came.
It was a moving service for it was a liturgical expression of all
that the trip meant to the youngsters and to the local parish. In
future years we always had a church service on the last night.

In the youth club the youngsters learned something about
belonging, and about the church caring about them and they
learned something of their own responsibility to the church. It
was a place where they found acceptance and were given value
by the church and by their peers. Friendships were made, some
of which I know have lasted to today. Our summer time away
helped to build up trust in the group and strengthened the life of
the youth club for the rest of the year. There were of course high
jinks and problems and incidents on our summer sorties to the
country, but never anything too serious. We didn't have many
rules but I did make one – that they were not to drink spirits
while they were away – and I don't believe it was ever breached.
Maybe this was because of a rider I added to the rule: that if I
saw anyone, or knew that anyone had been, drinking spirits I
would put them on the next bus home!

One year on the way to Kerry having a lunch break in the
Savoy Restaurant in Limerick a fourteen-year-old boy ordered a
beer and when I challenged him he informed me his father gave
him a beer every Sunday with his lunch. I told him I wasn't his
father and it wasn't Sunday. Thirty years previously I had been
in an orphanage two streets away. The Havergal was now
closed, but while I was there, every year I spent a day tidying the
churchyard of one of the city churches, St John's, with a work
party of boys from the orphanage. In those days I could not have

envisaged myself, thirty years hence, ordained and in the Savoy Restaurant having lunch and in charge of a group of youngsters on their way to clean up a neglected churchyard in Kerry. I have a sneaking suspicion Archdeacon Waller or Bifty would not have put their shirt on it either.

During my time in Stillorgan the Diocese of Dublin, Glendalough and Kildare undertook a project to commemorate the disestablishment of the Church of Ireland. They planned to build an old people's home, Glenindare, at Merrion Road. One night I told the youth club about this project and suggested that they had some responsibility to older people in the community and perhaps they would like to raise some money for Glenindare. They agreed readily and we set about organising a sponsored walk.

I nearly got cold feet when I thought about what my big mouth had let me in for. The average age of the youngsters was about fourteen. However, it was too late for they were enthusiastic. We set about planning a sponsored walk from Limerick to Dublin at the end of our summer excursion to clean up a neglected churchyard in Askeaton, Co Limerick. It was a journey of about 120 miles, and we agreed to aim to walk about 20 to 25 miles a day and end up in Stillorgan on a Sunday afternoon.

I approached my old friend P. D. Odlum and asked him if the firm would sponsor us for £100. He agreed immediately and on the strength of this I approached a number of other firms and ended up with sponsorship of £1,000, (€13,579 in today's money). Our next goal was to get fit for the walk itself, so we walked every Sunday afternoon between January and Easter. At the beginning there were about 50 youngsters and we started with five miles. On the day we reached 15 miles the heavens opened, and rather than a voice from God to say how much he approved of what we were doing, it rained cats and dogs on us and only 17 walkers finished. We continued to train until we could walk 25 miles. We achieved this just in time for our excursion to Askeaton, to clean up the graveyard.

At the end of ten days when we finished the job we sent the

non-walkers home and on Monday 17 young people set out from Limerick City to walk to Stillorgan. The Mayor of Limerick, Stevie Coughlan, started us off on the Dublin Road and there was a great sense of anticipation amongst the youngsters who had trained so hard. Although I had walked every Sunday on the training walks, I didn't walk on the real thing because I had to keep in touch by car with the walkers to be available for any problems that might arise, and to carry their belongings. I had arranged with Church of Ireland clergy along the route that they and some of their parishioners would provide a meal, a bath and bed and breakfast for the walkers. They did this willingly, and so well did they enter into the spirit of the project that, despite tiredness and the occasional blisters or sore feet, their enthusiasm encouraged the young people. The walk was covered by one of the national chat shows and people along the way supported us. Some lorry drivers, presumably having heard it on their radios, stopped to give us money

We were lucky with the weather and, everything having gone according to plan, we reached Stillorgan on Sunday afternoon. Archbishop Buchanan, the American Ambassador, who was a friend of a parishioner, the rector, parents and parishioners formed a welcoming party for us. The youngsters were so happy to have achieved their goal, parents were proud of their children and parishioners were delighted to be associated with the project. After the formal welcome by the VIPs we adjourned to the church and held a service of thanksgiving. This was the first project to raise money for Glenindare.

Marcus was an ideal rector for a curate of my temperament. I was older and I would like to think more mature than the average curate who came to the job straight from school and college and I had a reasonably diverse experience of people and of life in general. I believe that Marcus realised that the way to get the best from me, both for my own sake and for the parish's, was to give me the freedom to do things in my own way. I couldn't claim that I was either organised or disciplined, to say the least, but I had great energy and stamina and I worked all the hours God gave.

Despite working in my own way, I learned a great deal from Marcus Taylor, a humble and conscientious priest. By his example he taught me the importance of making the sick, the elderly and the needy a priority and he taught me how to deal with difficult situations. We went together one day to visit two elderly sisters, one of whom was notorious for her tongue. She soon launched into a tirade about a neighbour, but before she got properly into her stride Marcus said, 'It's time for our prayers,' and she was down on her knees praying before she knew it.

It is difficult to remember how my actual work, now that I was ordained, measured up to the expectation and anticipation I had all those years in the Havergal, Moyaliffe, the Harding, the mill and the flat. I do know, however, that despite the occasional frustrations that arise in any job one does, I was immersed in the parish. I loved the work with the young people and I was happy working with Marcus, but after four years in Stillorgan I began to think about the future, and at my age a parish of my own was the next move.

The archbishop of the diocese was Alan Buchanan. He had spent most of his ministry in the North of Ireland and had been an army chaplain in the Second World War. He had been dropped with airborne troops into Arnhem on the occasion of that notable military cock-up and defeat for British Forces. He had been Bishop of Clogher and was now Archbishop of Dublin. He was a sincere and kindly man who made a lot of effort to be kind to people. When he appointed a new Archdeacon of Dublin, he wrote to all the other senior clergy who might have felt they were in the running, saying kind things and explaining why he hadn't appointed them! For months afterwards the stock question clergy asked each other when they met was, 'Did you get a letter?' Buchanan's sincerity came through in the peculiarly slow, almost fawning, way he spoke. A colleague, a good mimic, was forever taking him off and frightened the wits out of clergy at the most inappropriate times. I'd hear, 'Every blessing, Kevin,' and, sure Buchanan was there, turn around to find he wasn't.

He used a desk diary and also carried a pocket diary but didn't always co-ordinate the two, with the result that he often double booked appointments and had cancel at the last minute. I phoned to make an appointment to talk to him about my future in the diocese and the possibility of a move. He arranged to meet me at the Synod Hall one afternoon before a 5 o'clock Diocesan Council meeting.

'Kevin, I think I should be able to meet you for half an hour, say half past four.'

So I rushed in at the last minute arriving at half past four and he was there talking to somebody, and he stayed talking to them until after ten minutes to five, and then came over to me and said:

'We'll have to be quick, Kevin, I have a Council meeting in five minutes.'

'Well,' I said 'Archbishop, if that's the case, we better leave it to another day. We had an appointment for half past four and I can't talk to you about what's on my mind in five minutes.'

I was cross and I walked away, so I never got to talk to him about the possibility of where I might go or what I was going to do next, and it didn't seem to worry him. He was none the less a popular archbishop. I have no doubt he thought I was arrogant. I wasn't, but I thought he was unfair. Later at some meeting when I asked a difficult question he accused me of being arrogant, and maybe I was, but his accusation enabled him to avoid answering the question. It doesn't go down well in the church to speak your mind, to ask awkward questions or to be critical of the top brass. They don't like it.

Shortly after this the Rector of Zion Parish, Rathgar, Canon Hilliard, who had been there for a long time, to everybody's surprise, went to Geashill, a small country parish in Meath diocese. I met him around this time and he said there was no point in him staying in his later years in a big parish like Zion when a move to a lighter duty parish in the country would suit him and make an opening in Zion for a younger man. Roy Warke who had been Rector of Drumcondra and North Strand was appointed to Zion.

He was a traditional, methodical and conscientious clergyman who had been only three years in Drumcondra. It was, however, a good move for him. When he announced in church that he was leaving and where he was going, some of the Drumcondra parishioners were angry that he should leave so soon. They felt that he thought their northside working-class parish wasn't good enough for him. I don't know if it is apocryphal or not that after he had told them in church that he was leaving he announced the next hymn – 'To Zion's hill I lift mine eyes!' He was later appointed archdeacon of the diocese and in dealings I had with him in that capacity I found him to be excellent. I felt he was a good second-in-command, but he was later elected Bishop of Cork and I lost track of him.

After Warke left Drumcondra I met a man called Coombe who was a leading layman in the diocese. He had been a parishioner in Limerick and I had known him slightly there when I was a boy. He had proposed to the Diocesan Synod the Glenindare project, the home the youth club did the sponsored walk for, and he had been a leading light in establishing it. He said to me, 'If you're interested in Drumcondra I'll propose your name.' I didn't say yea or nay. I didn't really want that parish as it had a name of being very Protestant and a tough place to work. Eventually Archbishop Buchanan called a Board of Nomination. The Board is the group selected from the parish and the diocese to nominate to the bishop a candidate as rector. After the meeting the archbishop phoned me three times and each time Jennifer gave me the message. After the third time I thought I had better phone him back.

'Kevin, I really must see you this evening, it's very important. There was a Board of Nomination today for Drumcondra. I was due to go to the ballet tonight but I have put it off so that you can come and see me.'

'Well, Archbishop, I have the Youth Club this evening and I haven't missed it in four years. I can't see you until after that.'

'What about at tea time?' he asked.

I agreed and went to see him. He told me what a good parish Drumcondra was and recounted all the great things about it.

'A wonderful parish, Kevin, a wonderful parish,' he said in his slow voice. I didn't quite see it his way and I knew it had an appalling rectory and I didn't feel like bringing my young wife into it. I certainly didn't want to have to confront the vestry about the rectory and I didn't want to go there.

'Ah,' he said, 'you'll see the nominators anyway?' These were the parishioners on the Board of Nomination.

'I really don't want to,' I said.

He said he thought I should, so I told him I would think about it over the weekend.

'And you'll pray about it.'

'And I'll pray about it.'

'And you'll come back to me after the weekend.'

He said this to me on the steps of the See House as I was leaving and I said to him:

'All I can say to you, Archbishop, is that the Holy Spirit would want to be working overtime if I'm to take that parish.'

I suppose that confirmed him in his view that I was an arrogant pup. So I went home and told Jennifer, who was a rock of sense. She made the point that there was a curate in the parish and it was unusual for a curate, as I was, to be appointed as rector to a parish with a curate. She also said that if I turned it down, I would never be offered a decent parish in Dublin again and it would be my own fault. That was on Friday. On Sunday afternoon I had a phone call from one of the parochial nominators to ask if I would see them. I told him I wasn't ready to meet the nominators.

'But, Mr Dalton, it's the unanimous wish of the nominators to see you.'

I suppose I was flattered, so I reluctantly agreed to see them.

'I'll fix these guys,' I said to Jenny.

Anyhow the three of them arrived, Arthur Garrett, Walter Hughes and Jack Kendall. When they sat down I said:

'Before we start what'll you have to drink?' One of them said immediately:

'God, I hope you come to us.' My ruse to put them off had

backfired and they began to tell me what a great parish it was. Among the impediments I brought up was the rectory. That would be no problem – they would put in central heating. I told them I certainly wouldn't bring my wife into it the way it was.

The usual course of events in those days when there was a good supply of clergy was that after a first curacy in Dublin a man went down the country to a small parish as rector and in due course came back to Dublin. The other possibility for me was to go north, but that was out because of my republican outlook. I couldn't cope with the Northern Protestants. Given my age, the fact that Jenny wasn't keen to go to the country, that the archbishop and I were both praying about it and it looked as if the Holy Spirit was indeed working overtime, on Jenny if not on me, I finally relented and accepted the nomination to Drumcondra.

There was some surprise among the senior clergy that a curate was appointed straight to a city parish. It was a breakthrough, as on the scale of things curates were people of little importance. Sam Poyntz, Vicar of St Ann's, said to his curate who was a friend of mine, 'I suppose Dalton is delighted with his appointment. He'll have his work cut out; it's the toughest parish in Dublin.'

For the service of institution the church was packed and there was a large number of clergy robed. Conscious of others who had worked in the parish over the years I chose as the first hymn 'For all the saints who from their labours rest'. Liturgy and the occasional offices of the Book of Common Prayer weren't my strong point, so I wasn't familiar with the service of 'Publick Institution of a Minister to a Cure' and when I knelt before the archbishop and in that slow sincere way he spoke he said:

'I Alan, by Divine Providence Archbishop of Dublin, Glendalough and Kildare, to our beloved in Christ, the Reverend Kevin Dalton, Clerk in Holy Orders, Bachelor of Divinity, Greeting.' I nearly laughed, thinking of the diocesan mimic. Furthermore there wasn't much Tudor English in use where I was brought up, and whereas I was used to it in the services of the church, as an integral part of the liturgy, it seemed strange to me to use it to address somebody in this way.

The service was impressive and Marcus preached the sermon, addressing the parishioners and saying 'Look after your new rector and he'll look after you.' Afterwards the parish put on the usual 'bun fight' of tea and cakes that ended with the usual speeches. The service and the tea afterwards with a couple of hundred people present is a tremendous support, and then you wake up the following morning to get on with the job and face the realities of running a parish on your own. There is a big difference between being a curate and a rector. As a curate you don't realise the responsibilities your rector is carrying, the decisions he has to make and the flack he has to take. As a curate you are the white-haired boy to most parishioners, but Marcus's last words to me leaving Stillorgan were, 'From now on, Kev, the buck stops with you.'

CHAPTER ELEVEN

Drumcondra, North Strand

Of the myriad of jobs a rector has to do it is inevitable that each rector is better at some than at others. Depending on temperament and personality, each rector will do some jobs well and some only averagely or even poorly. For some the new man by definition cannot be a patch on the old and for others he is by definition better than his predecessor. For some the present rector is always a candidate for crucifixion and when he leaves the parish he becomes a candidate for beatification. One parishioner of Drumcondra is reported as having said of me, 'If he spent less time lighting fires for little old ladies and more on preparing the liturgy for Sundays it would suit him better.' What he really meant was it would suit *him* better. It may have been fair comment. I found pastoral care and work with people easier than sophisticated liturgy. I enjoyed it and invested a great deal of myself in it. I had a curate for a short while when I went to Drumcondra first but he was appointed to a parish in Cork. On that first Christmas on my own I had to visit over 40 housebound people and another 20 in nursing homes and I brought around between 30 and 40 home communions.

Without a curate in the parish with two churches I had to reduce the number of services, and the extent of pastoral care was affected. The parishioners did not look kindly on this, but a fellow cannot divide himself in two. Most parishioners in a parish have no idea what the totality of a rector's job is. They are only aware of the bits that impinge on themselves. I had to point out that one man cannot possibly do the work of two. In order to silence some of the complainers one rare gem of a parishioner who understood, spoke at a parish meeting, held to discuss the absence of a curate, and challenged the ones who complained: 'If you want the rector to do the work of two men you will have to double his stipend.' This was the language they understood and the message began to get through. Not that I wanted a double stipend, but the point bore the reality in on those who didn't think.

These were the days when there was little coming and going or co-operation between Roman Catholic and Church of Ireland parishes and, as a small minority, Church of Ireland parishioners felt somewhat vulnerable, in some unthought out and inarticulate way, to a takeover. This was not helped of course by the cruel and inflexible implementation of the *Ne Temere* decree that took away from a mixed marriage couple the free exercise of their conscience to make the decision about the religious upbringing of their children and forced them to promise to bring them up as Roman Catholics.

There was a new block of flats built at the North Strand end of the parish where there was a great deal of unemployment. This was the area where the bombs fell that precipitated the evacuation of the children of Miss Carr's Home to Ballinacor. There were many children living in the area, and one day approaching Christmas a man called Sean from the Catholic parish approached me to ask if they could borrow our parish hall, which was in the grounds of North Strand church, to hold a Christmas party for the children.

'What about William Street?' I asked him, referring to the Catholic parish hall.

'It's booked out, and if you can't help us there's nowhere else to hold a party.'

I told him I would come back to him and consulted two churchwardens who agreed with me that we should lend the hall provided they were out by 6.00 pm as our evening service started at 7 o'clock. When I told Sean he was thrilled – the children would have their party. I didn't bargain for the uproar in the parish that ensued. I was accused of selling out to the Romans. It was a Roman takeover. One otherwise sensible woman said to me, 'O Rector, we're very worried with what you're doing with the parish.'

Later she called to Jennifer at the rectory and told her they were all desperately worried that on a Sunday especially the rector had given the hall to Roman Catholic people. Jennifer said:

'But the children wouldn't have any party if he had refused. They are underprivileged kids and haven't got much in life.'

'I don't care, they have their own hall.'

'But their own hall wasn't available, it was booked up.' Jennifer said, and then added, 'I wonder what Jesus would have done in that situation.'

The poor woman was struck dumb for a minute and then she said:

'You know Mrs Dalton, I never thought of it like that.' And she never mentioned it again.

The unthinking Protestant attitude would have been that although Protestants were all going to hell, they were good enough to borrow a hall from. Something like 'I think you're a worthless person, but will you lend me a fiver.' In this case this drew out an unChristian attitude from some parishioners. Later on at a parish meeting a woman was making a cryptic and convoluted point that was critical of me. So I interrupted her and said:

'What you really want to say is that you resent the fact that I lent the parish hall to Roman Catholic children to hold a Christmas party.'

'Yes,' she said.

'Well,' I said, 'I want every parishioner to understand something. As long as I'm rector of this parish if I can use parish facilities to help other people whoever they are, so long as it doesn't interfere with the life of the parish, I'm going to do it.' Jack Kendall, one of the nominators stood up and said in a determined voice, 'I'll back the rector 100 per cent on that,' and there wasn't another word about it, and before long local groups were welcome to use the hall when the need arose. Later on the woman who was so upset about the matter became an enthusiastic member of an ecumenical group in the area.

Early on I established contact with, and was warmly received by, the Roman Catholic clergy at All Hallows seminary. I always felt welcome there and they showed me great hospitality, despite our sometimes contentious debates. We were never artificially polite, but there was always a warmth and mutual respect evident in our discussions. I grew to value them as friends and they provided for me an oasis in which I could relax and be myself. A number of them came to my institution service when I moved to Monkstown.

My parish extended from Collins Avenue, through Drumcondra, North Strand and East Wall down to Alexandra Basin. In this area there were six or seven Roman Catholic parishes, but our main ecumenical contact was with Fr Matt Burke, a Corkman, parish priest of East Wall. He and I became good friends and shared pastoral problems. He once asked my advice about a difficulty he had with a curate.

'Well, Matt,' I said, 'I had a curate who was playing up and I gave him several chances, but eventually I had to tell him that if he still didn't do what I asked there would be no cheque at the end of the month.' I believe Matt followed a similar course and I heard afterwards that his curate soon angled for a move. The first time I invited Fr Matt to join us for an ecumenical service he accepted and told his parishioners that he would lead them, wearing his soutane, from St Mary's Church, up East Wall Road to North Strand Church on Sunday afternoon. He did just that and it was a strong symbolic gesture of ecumenical co-operation.

I never felt a sense of importance, nor was I aware of status, in my office as a clergyman. I felt no different than I felt at any time in my life. One day my predecessor was back in the parish and said to me, 'Well, Rector, how are you getting on?' I almost looked behind me to see who he was talking to and then realised some people saw the rector as a person of some standing. I never saw myself as such, but simply as a person with a job to do and a vocation to pursue.

My time in Drumcondra North Strand was as tough a seven years as I put in anywhere. I had great energy and stamina and I never stopped. Despite the difficulties and frustrations of running a parish there were a lot of good people who supported me and I found the work satisfying. During the tough times only a sense of humour saw me through. If you can't see the humour in some human situations you might as well pack up.

The Parish of Drumcondra North Strand had a preponderance of older people and consequently I had many more funerals than weddings or baptisms. In seven years in the parish I had over 200 funerals, and on more than one weekend I had three coffins in the church. One Thursday I was called to a nursing home to a parishioner who had just died. Later I called to her home to arrange the funeral with her son for the following Saturday. On Friday just before I left home to take a wedding I received a phone call to tell me another parishioner had died that morning. I went up quickly to the house and although the woman who died was old and her death was expected I met doom and gloom from the woman's daughter and her son the likes of which I had never encountered before. It seemed to me to be out of proportion. They weren't crying but their misery was palpable. It wasn't sorrow. It was total disaster. I was unable to get a word out of them or lift them or console them in any way. I asked where the burial would take place and they said they didn't know. They thought there was a grave but they didn't know where. I told them to search the house for the papers and I would call back later. I went off to the wedding and called back that evening and discovered two different people. It was as if the snow had melted and the sun was shining and it was the middle of June – they were smiling and light hearted and talkative. They had found the papers for the grave but what had wrought the transformation was that during their search they discovered a large box of banknotes, so now everything was possible. They had thought the funeral would put them in debt but now not only would it not cost them anything, the discovery of the money had put them very much in credit.

They wanted the remains to go to Drumcondra Church on Saturday afternoon. On the way up to the church on Saturday

morning to take the first funeral I got a call to say that someone
had broken into the school in North Strand and was going
berserk. As I arrived I saw a fellow climbing out over the wall
and running away. He was probably on drugs and he looked
like a wild animal. When I went inside he had ripped out all the
water pipes and the whole school was flooded. I had to get up
on the roof to tie up the ballcock. I was late for the funeral but
the people who looked daggers at me had no idea why. I took
the funeral and in the afternoon I arranged for somebody to look
after the school and then took the service of reception for the
woman with the box of notes under her bed.

That evening I got a call from Scotland from a parishioner to
say his wife had died there while on holiday. She had already
been cremated and her husband asked if he could bring her
ashes straight to the church from the airport later on that night
as he didn't want to have them in the house overnight. I agreed
and took the service of reception for the ashes. I went home and
struggled with a sermon into the small hours and then had the
full rota of services on Sunday, morning and evening.

On Monday morning I took the funeral service and burial at
Dean's Grange of she who had had no faith in banks. That afternoon the church was packed for the service for the ashes of the
woman who died in Edinburgh and I conducted the interment
service for them in Drumcondra churchyard. I was just into the
vestry, taking off my surplice when a parishioner burst in to say
that another parishioner had collapsed in the churchyard outside and they thought he was dead. I went out and he was. Next
day I took the service of reception and the following day the
funeral. After all of this I had no conscience in taking a few days
holiday.

Recounting this sequence of events gives a picture of how
busy one was over those days but it does not paint the picture of
the mental and emotional exhaustion that goes with supporting
families through these events. I had no idea when I was a boy in
Moyaliffe incubating a vocation to ordination what was involved, and despite it all I had no regrets.

In any parish you find the full spectrum of people in terms of their support for the rector or disapproval of or opposition to him or her. It is natural for people to find they agree with the attitudes or opinions of some people and not of others. In the matter of religion this is particularly so. Some people will support the rector no matter what and some will oppose the rector almost as a matter of principle because they don't really approve of him or her anyway. People's understanding and expectation of what a parish should be varies and different people understand their membership differently. Some people see it primarily as a gut loyalty to a particular tradition, others as a worshipping community providing spiritual sustenance and support for living in the world, and there is a variety of expectations in between. The one thing that almost all parishioners assume is that everybody ought to understand the parish as they do and of course this is never so, and life for the rector and the parish is often made difficult by the diversity of expectations that parishioners assume but seldom state. Often these expectations are felt and not thought out or articulated.

This was as true of Drumcondra, North Strand as of any parish. I had great support from some people and others seemed to oppose me at every turn. It is said that the most difficult vestries are those composed of people who in their working lives take rather than give orders and so, on the vestry where they have some power, they are determined to use it to the full.

The bane of my life, however, in the parish was not people but a churchyard. Before Glasnevin Cemetery was opened the churchyard of Drumcondra church was one of the main burial places on the northside of Dublin. Gandon, the architect of the Four Courts and the Custom House, is buried there in the grave of his friend Edmond Grosse, the antiquarian. They were friends and I believe made a pact to be buried in the same place. During my time the churchyard was almost full, and the only interments that took place were in family graves where there was still space.

Gerry was the sexton who looked after the churchyard but

when it came to making decisions it all came back to me. He maintained the graveyard well but there was little burial space left in it and, when it was necessary to rod a grave to see if there was room for a further burial, he always sent for me. To rod a grave is to push slowly a thin metal rod down until you feel the top of the first coffin lid from the surface to gauge if there is room for another burial. It was a sensitive operation – if the last burial had been relatively recent you could feel the resistance of the lid easily, but if the last burial had been a long time ago discerning the lid was not so easy and you might be into the coffin before you knew it.

I got a phone call one afternoon from an undertaker in the centre of the city to say that an aunt of one of my parishioners had died and the funeral would be going to Drumcondra, and he gave me the grave number. He told me a Mr Bannon, a cousin of my parishioner, was dealing with it.

'When is the funeral?' I asked.

'The day after tomorrow.'

'Well,' I said, 'you'd better hold off till we test the grave. Most of those graves are full.'

'Oh,' said the undertaker, 'there's no question about this one, the family tell me there's plenty of room.'

'Well,' I said, 'don't put the notice in the paper until I come back to you.'

The next morning I went up to Gerry and we tested the grave to discover that it was full. There was no room for a further burial and there is a law against burial too close to the surface. So I rang the undertaker pleased with myself that I had been proved right, but by this time he had inserted the death notice in the paper giving Drumcondra as the place of burial. He began to argue with me about what the family had said and then asked if they could have a new grave. I told him again that there were no new graves and only a few burials left in old ones and that this family's grave wasn't one of them. In the end he still wasn't satisfied and I told him that I was sorry but the funeral couldn't come to Drumcondra and they would have to make other arrangements.

I have no idea where they buried the poor woman but in a few days I got a letter from Mr Bannon demanding an explanation. The situation was perfectly simple and I had already taken a great deal of time to explain it to the undertaker. I was busy in the parish and I didn't have the time to become involved so I didn't answer the letter. He wrote again in the same vein and again I didn't answer. Then one day I met Archbishop Buchanan at an event and he said, 'Oh, Kevin, I've had a letter from a man called Bannon and he tells me you won't answer his letters. Would you ever write to him because he's tormenting me.' 'I will,' I said, but I hadn't got around to it before I met Buchanan again and he said, 'Kevin, you haven't replied to that man yet. He's been writing to me again.' So I wrote to Bannon and told him the reason I was writing was that the archbishop had asked me to and that he was making a very holy man's life a misery writing unnecessary letters about a simple matter that was over and done with. I then explained the law about burials and suggested that if he wasn't satisfied he should contact his solicitor. To my surprise I had a civil reply thanking me for my letter and there was no more about it. It was a lesson to reply promptly to letters which, however, I haven't learned yet.

There was a lovely old woman in the parish called Bella who never married and lived in one of the Corporation flats. Her people had been bookies and had fallen on hard times and lost a lot of money. She had a brother Bill who married a Catholic and reared all his family Catholics according to the promise he made when he got married. He was never seen in the Church of Ireland church from the day he married his wife until after he buried her over thirty years later. On the Sunday after his wife's funeral he was back in North Strand church and never missed a Sunday after that. He was an old-age pensioner and insisted on taking the envelopes to make his weekly contribution to the parish. When there was a meeting of parishioners to discuss the vestry's case that the parish could not afford a curate, Bill, whose sole income was his old age pension, said, 'I give 2/6d a week to the parish and I'm prepared to double it.'

Bella had worked as a cleaner in a flourmill. She had the same self-effacing but generous spirit that Bill had. One year I got her a supply of coal for Christmas from a church charity. She was most grateful, but in the New Year she told me she would never take the coal again because it should go to people who were worse off than she was. One Tuesday morning coming out of the church after a service Bill was sitting on a chair in the porch, hat on his knees, stick by his side waiting for me.

'Your reverence.'

'Yes Bill, what is it?'

'Ah,' he said and waved his hands over his head.

'What do you mean Bill?'

'Ah,' he said and did it again.

'I don't understand you Bill.'

'Ah,' he said, 'it's Bella.'

'What's wrong with Bella?' And he waved his hands over his head again.

'What are you trying to tell me Bill?'

'She's away in the head, she's roaring like a bull, the doctor's with her, you better come over.'

So I went over, by which time the doctor had sent for an ambulance and left. Bella was diagnosed as having cancer and after three weeks in hospital they sent her home and family began to appear from nowhere. Bella kept them waiting, for it took her three years to die. During this time Bill and her niece Mary, both of whom I came to know well, were good to her and did everything they could to look after her. I visited Bella regularly and became fond of her. She really was a saint – gentle, undemanding and so appreciative of all that Bill and Mary did for her. When she died I wasn't able to take the funeral. By then we had a curate and I asked him to take it. The family grave was an elaborate one commensurate with the family having seen better days – not the kind of grave in which you would expect to bury someone from Corporation flats.

I thought no more about Bella until one Saturday evening I was clipping the hedge at the front of the rectory. A small stout woman arrived, with an equally small stout man following a respectful two or three paces behind. I was on top of the stepladder clipping the top of the hedge and she looked up at me and said:

'Good afternoon, rector.'

' Do I know you?' I said.

'Oh,' she said 'I'm a parishioner.'

'I don't think I see you in church.'

'I'm a niece of Bella,' she said. Then I realised who she was and in the three years that Bella took to die I don't believe she visited her more than two or three times and I understood that Bella left this niece rather than Mary, the niece who looked after her, whatever few pounds she had.

'Well,' said I, 'what can I do for you?'

'I've come about the foxes.'

'What about the foxes?'

'The foxes that are going down into the grave and tormenting Bella.'

'The foxes couldn't be tormenting Bella for she's with her maker,' I said, 'And I'm quite sure of that.'

'Well, I want to put poison down to stop them.'

'You can't do that,' I said, 'there are often innocent dogs in the graveyard, and children sometimes play there and you might poison them.'

'Well,' she said, 'I'll put stones down the hole.'

'You can't do that either, and have the foxes digging more holes and tormenting some other poor misfortunate.'

'Well if that's your attitude,' she said, 'I'll go to the authorities.'

By this time I was down off the ladder, so I pulled myself up to my full height, looked her straight in the eye and said:

'I am the authorities.'

She turned on her heel and bounced off muttering, with the small stout man, by now red in the face, and not having opened his mouth, keeping his respectful two or three paces behind.

I got into my car and followed them up the road. I pulled in beside them and wound down the window.

'I suppose you're going to the Health Department.'

'The very place,' she says, 'first thing on Monday morning.'

'Well,' I said, 'you'll want to be careful because there are still some families, including your own, that have room for another burial in that churchyard and if they close it down I'll have to tell the other families why.'

She cocked her head in the air and walked off, the little man his usual few paces behind and I never saw sight nor sign of her again.

Drumcondra churchyard was an island of peace in the middle of a residential area. It was a little piece of *rus in urbe*, and I could understand why people wanted to be buried there, despite the foxes. However, some people have a strange sentiment about family graves. Damage or interference of any kind is taken personally and considered an affront to the family. Perhaps it is that since I don't have a family grave I don't understand the mystique that goes with one. It is well known that people of modest means when they become elderly will deprive themselves of even necessities rather than touch money they have put aside to bury them, perhaps for fear of burial in a pauper's grave.

There was a Mrs Mullarkey in the parish who had been a Roman Catholic and became a member of the Church of Ireland when she married many years before and reared all her children Church of Ireland. This was a courageous thing for her to do in the Ireland of those days. She was old now and a widow and she loved her Sunday morning service. Coming out of church one Sunday she pointed to one of three graves beside the wall near the sexton's house and said, 'That one's my grave, that's where I'll be going.' She said it in a simple and matter-of-fact way without a hint of morbidity. It was a great security to her to know where she would be buried. I tried to point out to her that I hoped she would be going further than a grave in Drumcondra churchyard. During the summer she used to go to the churchyard and cut the grass and keep the grave tidy.

In due course Mrs Mullarkey died and we buried her where

she always knew she would go. I missed her from church but I didn't think much more about her until about six months later. Jennifer was teaching and I was in the rectory on my own one Friday and had just sat down to my lunch when the doorbell rang. On the step stood a large woman in her mid-fifties, made up to the nines with a head of yellowy-red hair out of a bottle like the glow of the setting sun.

'I've come to see you about my daddy.'

'What about your daddy?' I said.

'He's buried above in the graveyard and he has been inter-fered with.'

'What do you mean "he's been interfered with"?'

'Someone's been at his grave.'

'Well,' I said, 'Gerry the sexton is the man to see about that.'

'Oh,' says she, 'Gerry's not responsible. You're responsible. You'd better come up.' So I left my lunch and up I went.

I suspected it might have been the foxes again but I waited for her to show me and hear what she had to say. The foxes used to go over the wall of All Hallows seminary next door to the bins outside the kitchen and bring back all they could get and they left bones strewn around the churchyard.

'Where's your daddy buried?' I asked.

'There,' she said, pointing to one of the three graves beside the wall. It was beside Mrs Mullarkey's grave, which accounted for some fresh soil lying around. Then she saw bones and began to cry. 'Look at that,' she said, pointing to the bones, confirmed in her view that her father's grave had been desecrated, and streams of mascara ran down her face. I explained to her about the foxes and the bones and tried to comfort her and to explain that burial in the graveyard was at the owner's risk since no-body had an automatic right to be buried there, it being a pre-1870 burial place. Only people with family graves and the ap-propriate document to prove it could be buried there. I told her all this to let her see what a privilege it was to have a grave in Drumcondra churchyard and to mitigate her cause for com-plaint. So to show her how seriously I was taking her I said:

'We'll test the grave and see if everything's all right.'

I called to Gerry's house to get the rod and he was just calming down after a session with the woman before she came to me. To demonstrate I pushed the rod slowly down the next-door grave and when the rod stopped I said:

'There's Mrs Mullarkey,' and I moved to the next one, 'And there's your daddy. It must have been a good coffin. How long has he been dead?'

'Forty seven and a half years.'

'Well Missus' I said 'I don't think I've seen you around here before. Do you come here often?'

'No,' she said, 'I've been up once since he died.'

'What in the name of God brought you?' I asked.

'I had a dream last night that someone was interfering with my daddy,' and she started to cry and the mascara began to run again.

'Well,' I said, 'the best thing you can do if you think something wrong has happened is to go to your solicitor and let him handle it, and if he writes to me I'll get the church solicitor to deal with it and then you and I can stay friends.'

I was absolutely fed up with the trouble I had with the churchyard and went home and phoned the Church Body solicitor, recounted the story and told him I was going to close the churchyard.

'You can't do that,' he said, 'as long as there are spaces left. If you get correspondence send it to me and I'll deal with it.' I heard nothing further for maybe six or seven weeks.

It was a Friday lunchtime and the doorbell rang. There she was in all her glory, same time, same place. Friday must have been her day off, and three or four steps below her was a young fellow in his twenties.

'My husband is up in the churchyard and he wants to talk to you about what happened my daddy.'

'Well Missus,' says I, 'the last time you came here I was trying to eat my lunch and when I came back it was ruined. I'm at my lunch now, and I'll come up when I've finished.' At that the young fellow lit up off the steps as if he had been stung by a nest of wasps and says:

'You're not fit to be a clergyman. I'll tear the collar off your neck.' So I said to her:

'Who is this civil young man?' knowing well who he was.

'That's my son,' said she.

'He's a very courteous young gentleman,' said I.

'You did so interfere with my grandaddy,' said the young man. So I said to him something I remember hearing as a child, though untrue:

'Do you know young man that if you struck me and you were found guilty in court you'd have to go to jail. You couldn't be fined or get probation. You must get jail if you strike a priest.'

'You did interfere with my grandaddy. I tested the grave myself.'

'Well you could go to jail for that too, interfering with the dead without authority.'

'And where are you from?' I asked the mother.

'Oldcastle, Oldcastle in the County Meath.' And I knew from the way she answered they were a bit mad or else they were after money, but whatever the reason on this occasion I was convinced it wasn't concern for her daddy.

So off they went and I ate my lunch and I never went up to see the husband. Early the next week I got a letter from her solicitor demanding to know what I had done to her daddy. I sent it on to the Church Body solicitor, and that was the last I heard of it.

* * *

Mixed marriages, or as we call them to-day inter-church marriages, were much more of a problem in those days than they are today. Even when new and more relaxed Roman Catholic regulations came out some conservative priests still insisted on the *Ne Temere* regulations concerning the upbringing of children.

John Moore and his wife were good parishioners of mine and regular churchgoers. Their sons, however, weren't gospel greedy. During the afternoon of the day on which Rob, one of these sons, was due to come to see me in the evening with his fiancée Peg to discuss their wedding, I met his mother May by chance.

' I believe they're going up to see you tonight, rector.'

'Yes,' I said.

'You'll be nice to them won't you?'

'Of course I will, what do you expect me to be, May?'

It was a cold November night and I had the fire lighting in the sitting-room. The doorbell rang and there was the young couple. Rob introduced me to his fiancée who was a pretty girl, but she looked worn out, pale and apprehensive. They came in and sat down and after the usual pleasantries they told me they were getting married in the Catholic church and would I come to the wedding. I said that of course I would provided Rob's rights as partner and prospective father were honoured, as I'm sure they would be. We talked for a while. They told me how they met and how long they had known each other and then I made coffee. While we drank our coffee Peg told me she was pregnant. A mixed marriage and the bride pregnant was starting at somewhat of a disadvantage so I made nothing of it but tried in conversation to let them know that I would support them in any way I could. We finished our coffee and off they went.

About an hour later the doorbell rang. They were back, and asked if they could come in for a minute. Inside Peg asked me:

'Would you marry us in North Strand church?'

'I thought you were getting married in your own church.'

'You remember I told you when you asked me that I had been to see my priest. Well what I didn't tell you was that when I called it was a filthy cold wet night and the priest left me standing on the doorstep and went inside and returned with a piece of paper and said: "Sign here." When we got home after leaving you tonight I was telling my father how nice you were to us and that you were prepared to support us, so I told him "I'd like that man to marry me". Daddy said, "I don't care who marries you so long as you're married in church".'

'Of course I'll marry you but you'd better get your parents to come and see me in the morning.'

Peg's parents had a small shop a couple of miles from North Strand and they both arrived down to the rectory next day. I explained to them that as Peg had already been to see the priest to make arrangements to be married in his church he might not be too pleased that she had changed her mind and now wanted me to marry her in North Strand church. I pointed out to them that some years earlier there had been trouble in Fethard-on-Sea, Co Wexford over a mixed marriage when businesses had been boycotted. I told them I didn't think it was likely, but I'd hate anything like that to happen to them. However, if the priest got upset and made an issue of it things could be difficult. I emphasised that I didn't want to score points, but since Peg had asked me I would marry her if they were happy about it.

'We're happy,' they said. 'We know the priest. We go regularly to Mass there and we'll go and see him.'

I married Peg and Rob three weeks later in North Strand church. They were happy and their families were happy, and at the reception Peg's father came over to me and bought me a drink.

'Mr Dalton,' he said, 'you were right about the priest.'

'What do you mean ?'

'Well in the event I didn't go to see him, since you told me he'd get notice of the wedding and he did. A week or two later he arrived up to the house and created fair hell. He threatened me and said that if I didn't get Peg to change her mind he'd excommunicate the whole family, and I did a thing I never thought I would do in my life. I opened the door and said to the priest of the church I love, "Father there's the door," and that wasn't the end of it. He arrived up yesterday and said "I've come to tell you you only have 24 hours to save your souls".'

After Peg had her baby she came to see me to tell me she wanted to have the baby baptised in the Catholic church because her parents were so supportive of her. I told her I understood completely and that if the priest were to invite me I would be happy to be present at the baptism. To my great surprise I was invited, but soon realised it was a different priest.

This was towards the end of the difficult times for mixed marriages which these days normally take place in the church of the bride, whichever religion that is, and the clergy of the other partner normally take part in the ceremony. The Protestant partner does not make any promise about the upbringing of the children and the Catholic partner makes a conditional promise.

* * *

We sometimes hear people say: 'So and so is a saint.'

'Ma, what's a saint?'

'A very holy and religious person.'

'And Ma, what's a martyr?'

'Someone who has to live with a saint!'

In the ministry you sometimes have the privilege of meeting a saint, but not that kind of saint. There was one in the North Strand end of the parish called Willie. He lived on his old-age pension, and was crippled with arthritis and confined to a wheelchair so I used to bring him the sacrament every month. Willie had been married and his wife had died at the birth of their only son. He wasn't able to look after the baby so his brother and his wife in England had brought him up. When I came to know Willie he was getting on in years and his son was grown up and living in England. His Catholic neighbours used to keep an eye on Willie and help him in whatever way they could. One day when I was with him I said:

'Willie, you must be very lonely on your own.'

'I'm not a bit lonely, sure I'm not on my own, the Lord Jesus is with me all the time.'

On another occasion just before Easter I had brought communion to him and I was sitting chatting when he took from a drawer the Bishops' Appeal envelope to give me. The Bishop's Appeal is the Church of Ireland fund that supports Third World emergency and relief work.

'Ah Willie,' I said, 'you shouldn't be bothering about that, you have enough to do to look after yourself.'

'Well rector, Almighty God has been very good to me, and I

decided that this lent I would go off vegetables and give what I saved to the Bishops' Appeal.'

When Willie died there were a few neighbours at his funeral and a bishop who happened to be in the parish for another service. I told him about Willie and added, 'Only God knows who the real saints are.'

Bishops can be out of touch with this kind of thing.

CHAPTER TWELVE

Monkstown

That was Drumcondra North Strand. I preached my farewell sermon on the seventh anniversary of the service of my institution. The parish had lived up to its reputation as a tough parish and I had worked hard there. I had contributed everything I could in pastoral care, ecumenical outreach and strengthening the sacramental life of the parish. It was rewarding to hear later on that when they came to look for a successor these were the emphases they wanted in their next rector. For a while before I left Drumcondra I was on the look out for a change. I knew the right thing to do was to move on. Furthermore, by now Jenny and I had two small daughters, Tara and Sally-Ann, and there was no back garden and the front garden was no more than a postage stamp. There were 18 rooms in the house, one large, one reasonable and the rest were tiny. It was on the corner of a busy road and wasn't a suitable house in which to bring up our two little girls. I considered going to a country parish but Jenny wasn't keen. Despite being a country girl herself she liked living in the city.

I had been approached some time earlier to allow my name to go forward for a Dublin suburban parish I would have been glad to go to. I even met the nominators but knew I hadn't done well with them. One of them was an old county type and I knew I wouldn't have suited him. None the less I held out a hope they might appoint me and when Archbishop Buchanan phoned to tell me I had not been appointed, he said, 'Kevin, I want to assure you that from the point of view of the diocesan nominators you will be one of the leading contenders for the next major parish that comes up in Dublin.' This was reassuring, but since he had a reputation for wanting to be kind and to make people feel good, I wasn't sure that my standing with the diocesan nominators was as good as he suggested.

The lay diocesan nominator at the time was a parishioner of Stillorgan where I had been curate so I went to see him to talk over my interest in a move. He discussed with me all the possibilities and he went through the Dublin parishes that were likely to become vacant in the near future. One by one I discounted them as not being for me. Having made what I considered a success of Drumcondra North Strand I felt I was entitled to one of the better parishes. I was, I suppose, in those days still a bit bigheaded; maybe the archbishop had been right after all. On reflection, however, after seven years in Drumcondra, I had a realistic understanding of what the parochial ministry was about.

Billy Wynne was rector of Monkstown at the time. He was about sixty and looked as if he would be there for life, so Monkstown had not been mentioned. To everybody's surprise he was appointed to St Ann's in Dawson Street, he said under pressure from the archbishop.

Being an experienced poker player it wasn't in my nature to show my hand, but I was interested in Monkstown. I was aware that there would be many others interested too and many of them senior to me.

The first inkling I got that the Monkstown parochial nominators might be well disposed towards me was one Sunday when two of them turned up in North Strand church to a Sunday morning service. Now it is traditional that parochial nominators 'spy' on possible rectors by going anonymously to services to see how he or she conducts the service and preaches in their present parish. They take you by surprise so you cannot put on a show. You might suspect if you saw two likely looking strangers sitting at the back trying to look inconspicuous or you might not. Fortunately for me they came on a Sunday when there was a service of enrolment for members of the 'Explorers,' a junior section of the Girls' Brigade, and also a baptism, so the church was full and there were people there who would not be out on a normal

Sunday. I meant to point this out to them later, but I forgot! After I had baptised the infant I brought it up to the front to the little 'Explorer' girls and talked about Moses in the bulrushes and the whole service came together well.

As the two nominators left the church they grinned and asked me if I knew who they were. I said I didn't and they didn't enlighten me. A couple of days later I had a phone call from one of them who declared he was one of the two strangers who had been at North Strand Church on Sunday. He asked me directly was I interested in allowing my name to go forward for Monkstown. I said I was, but I would like to know more about the parish first and I invited him to come and see Jennifer and me.

The nominator was Jack Teggin, a man of integrity, who gave me all the encouragement he could without giving me false hope. He was straight and honest about Monkstown parish, giving what he saw as its weaknesses as well as its strengths. I told him I thought it would not be easy to follow Billy Wynne and he replied, 'Don't worry about that. Every man going into a new parish will make it his own in due course.'

A couple of Sundays later the other two Monkstown nominators, Charlie Mitchell and Brian Taylor appeared in church to have a look at a prospective candidate for their parish. After I was appointed I met the Archdeacon who had been talking to Charlie Mitchell during the week following his visit to Drumcondra, and had asked him how the search was going.

'The search is over,' he replied. On the morning of the meeting of the Board of Nomination Charlie Mitchell phoned me:

'Mr Dalton, are you still interested in Monkstown Parish?'

'Yes,' I said, 'I am.'

'There's a Board of Nomination meeting tonight. If you are nominated will you accept?'

'I will,' I said, 'but I have one or two reservations.'

'What are they?'

'The rectory is one.'

'I can understand that,' Charlie said, 'but I assure you that the vestry will do everything, within reason, to bring that house up to standard, and if that isn't enough we will find a suitable house to replace it.'

'The other is that if I am appointed I would like not to have to tell the parish until after Christmas.' That of course was not possible, as a secret in the Church of Ireland is telling only one person at a time.

In the context of seniority and of the way of politics in the diocese, I was not the most likely candidate to get Monkstown. When you are keen to be appointed to a parish the date and time of the meeting that will make the decision are etched on your mind. It was 19 December 1979 at 4.00 pm. Jennifer was in Donegal with her parents, so I stayed within reach of the phone. When 5 o'clock came I was sure that someone else had been appointed so my curate and I went out to collect the last few items we needed to fill Christmas hampers for needy people. We arrived back to the rectory sometime after six o'clock and at about half past six the phone rang. It was Tom Salmon, who was one of the diocesan nominators, the same who had been so good to me when he was at St Ann's and had helped me with Hebrew when I was at Trinity:

'May I be the first to congratulate you?' So I knew I had arrived. Some short time later Archbishop McAdoo phoned to tell me the news officially. He was the slightest bit miffed that I already knew.

'I take it you will accept,' he said. And I of course said I did. I phoned Jenny to tell her the news and she was delighted, not least because we would not have to leave the city. The One who looked after me in Miss Carr's, in the Havergal and ever since was at it again.

The occasion merited a celebration so after I put down the phone having spoken to Jenny I opened a bottle of brandy I was keeping as a present for a friend, and the curate and I sat down and had a couple of drinks. The curate, who wasn't a drinker, rolled home with about two hours to spare before he was due to take a confirmation class. His wife was shocked to see him in such a condition and poured black coffee into him to have him ready to instruct some of the next generation of young Church of Ireland parishioners in the doctrines of the faith.

I announced at services on the next Sunday that I had been appointed to Monkstown and would be leaving the parish. The following week I went to bring communion to an old house-bound parishioner, Bunt Ebbs. She was the last of a family that had been in the parish for generations. I had been trying to per-suade her to put her name down for a nursing home to prepare for the time she could no longer live at home, and every time I mentioned it her response was the same:

'Ah sure I wouldn't want to leave my parish.'

As I entered the room instead of the usual smile and warm welcome she gave me a sideways glance and looked away. I went over and sat down beside her, put my arm around her and asked:

'What's wrong, Bunt?'

'You might have stayed till you buried me anyway.'

After I had gone the same Bunt refused to acknowledge that I had left the parish, and she kept sending me messages that I hadn't been to see her. She eventually ended up in a nursing home on Clonliffe Road and one day I was over in that direction I called to see her. She was the only Church of Ireland person in a large ward, and when she saw me coming the first thing she said was, 'I'm glad you came, it helps to keep the others at bay.'

Just before I was appointed to Monkstown Scruffy, our beloved wirehaired dachshund that had been given to us by the parishioner in Stillorgan as a wedding present 13 years previ-ously, died. Ethel, the Drumcondra churchwarden who was in charge of arranging a presentation from the parish, asked me what I wanted. Conscious of the low esteem I was held in by my bank manager, and the expense of moving house, I told her I'd be glad of the money.

'Be reasonable, rector,' she said, 'we will have to have some-thing tangible to give you for a presentation.'

'Well what about a cheque?' I said.

'I'll tell you what I'll do,' Ethel replied, 'I'll go and buy something for your new home.'

'Well,' I said, 'if you're happy to collect money from parishioners for a presentation to your rector and then go out and spend it what way you choose, on your own conscience be it.'

'Ah, rector, you're not being very helpful.' So I relented and said:

'All right, I'd like a dachshund puppy.'

'What?' she almost shouted at me. 'We couldn't possibly present you with a dog.'

'Why not?' I said, 'It's what I want.' I suppose she felt she couldn't inscribe a brass plate and attach it to a dog.

At the heel of the hunt Ethel gave in and on the night she presented me with a cheque and, to the surprise of those present and to the 'oohs' and 'aahs' of the animal lovers, also with a beautiful little dachshund puppy. We called him Pee, with good reason, and we had him for twelve years.

The night of the service of institution was a dark February night. As I drove down Monkstown Road the floodlit church came into view. It is a significant building architecturally and a landmark in the area. It gave me a good feeling that this parish would be my next challenge. I had some sense that I had earned it simply because over the previous seven years I had put so much into my last one.

From my dealings with the Monkstown nominators, especially concerning the rectory, I knew that the vestry and its sub-committees were a practical and sensible group of people that I could work with. After my appointment they set about renovating the rectory and consulted Jennifer and me and incorporated practically everything we suggested into their plans. The renovation was a major job and included bringing the kitchen up from the basement, and so we continued to live in Drumcondra for a number of months until all the work was completed. They didn't skimp on anything and did their best to make the house as comfortable a family home for us as possible. It was, however, an added strain running a new parish from the other side of the city, travelling over and back at least once every day.

Shortly after we moved into Monkstown rectory, one day I was running down the stairs to my study in the basement to watch a race on television. I stepped on a pool that Pee had piddled at the bottom of the stairs and went down like a stricken stag on the hard tiles of the basement floor and broke my leg in three places. I never did see the race, and spent the following six weeks running the parish from my hospital bed or with my leg up at home. I often wondered if Ethel, who had been reluctant to give me a puppy, had heard.

Though it is now twenty-two years since I was appointed to Monkstown, with a few more to go before I retire, my arrival in Monkstown completed a circle in an unexpected way. During my first few years in the parish one of my jobs as rector was that of chaplain to an orphanage, Glensilva, almost opposite the rectory on Monkstown Road. Formerly Miss Smylie's Home, this was the orphanage where Paul McGrath, the Irish international footballer, had spent some of his early life. Sometimes I would look at the children, with their lives stretching before them, and wonder whether any of them, having a similar beginning to my own, would have as fortunate a life as mine.

Afterword

So there you have it. I've had a rich and fulfilling life to date and see no reason why what's left to me, be it long or short, should not be the same.

It is hard to escape the conclusion that if my mother, a Roman Catholic, had entered a Roman Catholic home during her pregnancy I would have been taken from her and given for adoption, probably to America. I might have been brought up in a secure family, had a conventional education and have done a conventional job. I might, on the other hand have been adopted by a family that developed difficulties that created insecurities that caused me all kinds of problems. These and many other possibilities are the 'might-have-beens'.

I do not know why my mother, a Roman Catholic, went into the Bethany Home, a Church of Ireland home for unmarried girls, rather than to a Roman Catholic one. With the knowledge we have today I can only speculate that she knew something about the Catholic homes and how young women were treated in them. As things were she kept me herself for two years and it seems likely she knew that if she went to a Magdalen Home her baby would be taken away and given for adoption and so it seems she was determined that this would not happen. In a Church of Ireland home she was able to keep her baby, though no doubt she was put under great pressure to give me for adoption as the best thing for my sake and for her's.

It was perfectly natural that she had me baptised in a Roman Catholic church. It was extremely courageous of her to keep me and to try to get on with her life as, what we call today, a single mother. It is difficult to envisage today what a courageous deci-

189

sion that was in the Ireland of the 1930s. The all-pervading religious climate of those days turned an unmarried mother into a
pariah, somebody to be ostracised, shunned or at best pitied.
This was true in both the Catholic and Protestant communities,
as clergy of both traditions would generally have been strong in
their advice that a pregnant, unmarried woman should leave
her own community. My mother managed as best she could by
having someone to mind me while she was working and after
two years of what in those days must have been a great struggle,
both socially and financially, she finally gave up and placed me
in Miss Carr's Home. She visited me regularly there and took me
out for afternoons and I like to think that she intended to take
me home again when she got on her feet.

As things happened she did not do this. I never saw her
again after I went to the Havergal in 1941. Something transpired
in her life that made her change her mind. What that was I can
only speculate. It is likely she met somebody and didn't declare
that she had a son and as she became involved it became impossible for her to tell for fear she might lose the person she loved.
Or having fallen in love she may have told the man she loved
about me and he was not prepared to have her if I was part of
the package. There are of course other possibilities but whatever
happened I do not blame her. The pressures on her from the beginning must have been tremendous and the fact that in the climate of the time she kept me for two years and kept in touch for
a further seven years after that are a measure of her independence, her strength of mind and her courage.

During my early life I accounted for my parents to people,
when it became necessary, by saying they had gone to England
to work during the war and of course there were air-raids. One
weekend after I came to Dublin I took the ferry and wandered
around Liverpool in vague pursuit of this fantasy. I walked
around the city and on the Sunday morning I stopped a number
of people to ask the time of church services and was astounded
that most of them looked blankly at me and none of them knew.
I came back on the next boat without having achieved anything.

I left it there and did nothing further and subsequently never felt the need to try to trace my mother. Whereas I do not know what happened to her in the end I do know that she was not confined to a Magdalen Laundry and I cherish the hope that she led a fulfilled life.

The psychologists tell us that the experience of the first five years, or even less, of our lives influence or well nigh determine whether we grow up with a secure personality or not and influence the kind of adult we become. For the first two years of my life I was with my mother and between the age of two and the age of nine I spent in Miss Carr's Home where there was a secure routine and where I received a lot of love and a lot of care. Apart from being a member of a happy family, to be in Miss Carr's Home was the best possible place I could have been. My personality was formed and the benefits of this security were there before I went to the Havergal and had to endure all I have described of that institution and the people who ran it.

I do not want what I have said to be used as a judgment of the Roman Catholic Church, its priests, brothers and nuns who ran orphanages and homes for unmarried mothers in the early years of the State. I do not want anyone to think that I am saying that if I had been in a Roman Catholic orphanage it would have been all bad and because I was in Church of Ireland orphanages it was all good. This is not the case; life, at times, in the Havergal was no picnic.

I lived in two orphanages. In the first which was run by women there was a lot of love for the children and a lot of care. God as a loving Father and the love of God as seen in the Bible accounts from the gospels pervaded the religious teaching and were evident in the way we were treated, while the teaching of the Church of Ireland was passed on to us too. The second orphanage which was run by men was tougher and at times brutal and the Bible and Anglican Church teaching were still the basis of what we learned in religion classes, but the putting of the loving aspect of it into practice was much less evident and at times absent. Of one thing I am certain: there was no sexual abuse in either Miss Carr's Home or in the Havergal. The only sexual activity I was aware of were my own childish explorations in the wardrobe in Miss Carr's Home with the girl who was as curious as I was about the mysteries of *la différence!*